WAY-SIDE GLIMPSES,

North and South.

BY LILLIAN FOSTER.

NEW YORK:
RUDD & CARLETON, 130 GRAND STREET,
(BROOKS BUILDING, COR. OF BROADWAY.)
MDCCCLX.

STEREOTYPED BY
T. B. SMITH & SON,
82 & 84 Beekman-street.

Introductory.

R. G. Horton, Esq. :—

My Dear Sir :—

Accustomed to appeal to you upon occasions when I am perplexed with difficulties, I ask at this juncture, Can there not be a book without a preface as well as a church without a bishop? Besides, I do not know *how* to write a preface, and I also feel a shrinking modesty from addressing the public face to face. You know how these letters were written, and why they are published. You know, too, that life has been a sterner battle to me than usually falls to the lot of woman; but you also know that I have never shrunk from its cares, or thrown upon others the responsibilities which belonged to myself. Left alone, to "struggle with outrageous fortune" and retain for myself and family a respectable position in society, I have employed my pen to attain what Agar so beautifully describes as neither poverty nor riches. To this end I have collected these scattered letters, written at different periods dur-

ing the last few years, and mostly to the journal with which you have been so long associated. I think the position and advantages I enjoyed at the time they were written, afforded me superior opportunities to observe all the phases of scenery and society at the locations of my sojourn, which I have endeavored to portray with vivacity, accuracy, and impartiality.

I have hoped these communications would impart both instruction and pleasing interest to the public, in relation to the various routes of travel, as well as the places of fashionable resort for artists, statesmen, and men of business, with their families, during the pleasant season of the year, thus furnishing those who design to journey in the United States—whether American or foreigner—a synopsis of pleasant routes with the rendezvous of intelligent and refined travelers.

My aim has been to embrace as much of useful information as practicable, and to render the letters familiar and entertaining. Literary superiority I do not claim for them; but the information contained in the volume, and its low price, will, I trust, be inducements for readers to possess it.

I can not too gratefully express my acknowledgments to gentlemen and ladies all over the Union, and particularly at the South, for the kind-

ness and attention they have bestowed upon me. Particularly to the gentlemen of the press am I indebted for numerous favors, and to none more than you, my dear Sir, whose sympathy and aid has ever been so generously given, and to whom I now take the liberty to dedicate these "Way-Side Glimpses North and South," as the only testimonial I have to offer you of my esteem and friendship.

Very gratefully,

And sincerely, yours,

LILLIAN FOSTER.

NEW YORK, Sept. 19, 1859.

CONTENTS.

I.

PAGE

SUNDAY IN NEW YORK, ... 13

II.

RURAL SIGHTS AND SOUNDS IN DUTCHESS COUNTY, ... 20

III.

ANNUAL EXHIBITION OF THE AMENIA SEMINARY.—PLEASURES OF RURAL LIFE, ... 24

IV.

VISIT OF REV. DR. WAINWRIGHT.—REV. MR. FRISSELL.—THE OLD STONE CHURCH AT DOVER.—A CHARADE, ... 29

V.

THE WARM WEATHER.—AN AMUSING INCIDENT.—THE BEAUTIFUL EVENING, ... 36

VI.

LIFE AT WATERING PLACES.—THE PEQUOT HOUSE.—OUR BOARDERS, ... 42

VII.

PAGE

NOTES OF NOTABLE PEOPLE AND MATTERS IN CONNECTICUT,........ 47

VIII.

THE SOUND.—THE ABORIGINES.—PLEASURE SEEKERS.—HON. JOHN COTTON SMITH,........ 54

IX.

LEAVE-TAKING.—REVOLUTIONARY REMINISCENCES.—FASHION AND DISPLAY.—THE NORWICH STEAMERS,........ 60

X.

NIAGARA FALLS.—THE SUSPENSION BRIDGE.—THE LUNA BOW.—THE CLIFTON HOUSE,........ 66

XI.

GROWTH OF ILLINOIS.—MICHIGAN CENTRAL RAILROAD.—THE CHICAGO BREAKWATER.—THE TREMONT HOUSE.—EMIGRATION,........ 70

XII.

TRIP TO CHARLESTON.—THE VOYAGE BY STEAMER.—THE CHARLESTON HOTEL.—SLAVERY.—THE ARSENAL.—THE CITADEL ACADEMY,........ 78

XIII.

VISIT TO COLUMBIA.—NORTHERN AGGRESSIONS.—BEAUTIFUL WEATHER.—SOUTHERN RAILROADS,........ 86

XIV.

PAGE
Augusta.—The City Hall.—The Church of the Atonement.—Augusta Hotel, ... 90

XV.

En Route for Savannah.—A Southern Sunset.—Loss of Baggage.—The Pulaski Monument.—A "Slave" Funeral, ... 99

XVI.

Columbus.—The Legend of Lover's Leap, &c., ... 111

XVII.

A Trip to St. Louis.—Detroit.—The Towns of Michigan.—Chicago.—Illinois.—Prairies.—St. Louis, ... 119

XVIII.

Western Railroads.—The Hoosiers.—Filthy Cars.—Advice to Conductors.—Indiana.—Louisville.—Its Growth.—Politics.—Louisville Hotel, ... 129

XIX.

A Visit to Frankfort.—The State Capitol.—The Cemetery. — The Military Monument. — Daniel Boone.—Governor Morehead, ... 135

XX.

Steamboat Traveling.—Southern Scenery.—Southern Hospitality.—Growth of New Orleans, ... 146

XXI.

PAGE

THE SAINT CHARLES.—NEW ORLEANS IN WINTER.—A FASHIONABLE LADY'S DAILY ROUTINE.—MRS. GENERAL GAINES.—THE NEW CUSTOM HOUSE.—FREE SCHOOLS, 152

XXII.

DOWN THE MISSISSIPPI. — NEW ORLEANS. — A BAL MASQUE,........................ 161

XXIII.

VICKSBURG.—MISSISSIPPI STEAMBOATS,................ 167

XXIV.

MEMPHIS.—ITS BANKS AND BACHELORS.—THE LADIES. —WORSHAM HOUSE.—WAITING FOR A BOAT.—MISS MURRAY.—LEFT.—OFF,............................ 174

XXV.

NASHVILLE.—THE STATE CAPITOL.—UNIVERSITY OF NASHVILLE.—THE HUME HIGH SCHOOL.—CITY HOTEL,.... 180

XXVI.

RAINING DOWN AT NIGHT IN NEW YORK. — THE SAINT NICHOLAS HOTEL.—ITS EXTENT AND MAGNIFICENCE,.. 193

XXVII.

POLITICS IN ILLINOIS. — PROSPECTS OF CHICAGO. — NEW BUILDINGS, &c.,................................ 200

XXVIII.

PAGE

IN NEW YORK AGAIN.—GENIN'S BAZAAR,............ 207

XXIX.

GROWTH OF CHICAGO. — COMMERCE. — FASHION, &C.— NOMINATION OF HONORABLE R. S. MALONY FOR CONGRESS. — SPEECHES OF COLONEL RICHARDSON AND COLONEL CARPENTER. — THE FIFTH AVENUE OF CHICAGO,.. 212

XXX.

ILLINOIS POLITICS. — MR. DOUGLAS. — MR. LINCOLN.— COLONEL CARPENTER.—THE RESULT OF THE PRESENT CONTEST,.................................... 218

XXXI.

A TRIP TO THE WHITE MOUNTAINS. — THE FLUME HOUSE,.................................... 224

XXXII.

THE FLUME.—THE CASCADES. — THE OLD MAN OF THE MOUNTAINS,.................................... 228

XXXIII.

MONTREAL.—THE VICTORIA TUBULAR BRIDGE,.......... 234

XXXIV.

TRIP FROM CHICAGO.—RAILROADS.—PENNSYLVANIA CENTRAL.—THE ALLEGHANIES.—SCENERY.—THE ST. NICHOLAS HOTEL,.................................... 243

I.

Sunday in New York.

NEW YORK, July 1, 1853.

CIVILIZATION furnishes few more interesting or fruitful phenomena than the Sabbath in a large city, especially one composed of a mixed population like ours—each nation and class preserving its own peculiarities of manner and amusement, which on Sunday alone have an opportunity of development and indulgence. In the country, Sunday is a season of man's absolute repose, especially to the muscle-straining and sweat-producing classes, while in the city it is the schemers and thinkers alone that rest and refresh their consciences by religious exercises; while the great body of the hard-working population—the bone and sinew of the community—rush out, like children let loose from school, to enjoy a brief interval of excitement, and to inhale a few breaths of untainted air. Those whose days and hours are all their own, and who never by any possibility penetrate into the filthy and noxious quarters of the city, where helotism swelters in its rags and dirt, half suffocated amid poisonous vapors, can form but a poor idea of the preciousness of a few hours of relaxation, change of scene and pure air, to the laboring classes. To them the city is one vast prison, in whose trenches and passages they work and dig, with the privilege of escape and respite one day in seven. To them, Sunday is not only morally, but physically, a Sabbath; and civilization is beginning to discover that all real melioration of the condition of mankind must commence at the material side of the question. There is, doubtless, earnest and true devotion in the unconscious gladness of the laboring man who, with his wife and family, on Sunday, escapes from the city's walls, and feels himself walking and breathing in the free air of the heavens, perfumed with the breath of grove and field. The cheerful talk and happy laughter of these people are hymns and thanksgivings to the Creator, doubtless as acceptable as the richly-paid quartettes and nicely-modulated voluntaries, sandwiched with stereotyped prayers and sermons, which ascend from innumerable costly and magnificently-appointed churches.

New York is admirably situated for the accommodation of its working classes with the facilities for getting out of town and into the country. Perhaps there is not another instance in the world where the inhabitants in the middle of a city of six hundred thousand population can, in fifteen minutes, and at an expense of sixpence down to two cents, transport themselves literally into the country, surrounded by all the agreeable influences of woods and green fields, and soothed by that sense of silence and repose for which the heart of the citizen pines and his frame aches. If you would get a proper appreciation of the value set upon fresh air by those who get it but once a week, go to Hoboken on Sunday morning, and wander about its romantic retreats. At length, you will find yourself at the Elysian Fields—a beautiful spot, turfed with unbroken green, and shaded by majestic old trees, without a suspicion of under-brush. After drinking in the strength and rest lavishly imparted by the calm solitude of this lovely spot, and feeling as much renewed as Antæus when he had kissed his mother earth, you can walk leisurely down the splendid graveled water terrace along the banks of the river, listening to the sleepy murmur

> "Of the small ripple spilt upon the beach,"

and following with your eye the countless sails that, like a flock of gigantic white-winged creatures, glide through the far distance, with just sense of motion and life to give assurance that you are still in the actual world, but not sufficient to disturb the current of your dreamy reveries. Away to the left, and northwardly as far as the eye can pierce, stretches the dark outline of the monster city, coiled along the edge of the water in gigantic folds—now, at this safe distance, silent and asleep for you. As you gaze upon the gloomy labyrinth from which you have for a moment escaped, a sense of triumph and freedom comes over you that almost compensates for a week of toil.

In the city itself, the Sabbath is not without its peculiarities and excitements. It is true that Wall street is as still and silent as if it had been seized with an ossification of its granite heart, and the footfall of the solitary pedestrian echoes startlingly, like Layard's, as he penetrated into the unburied site of Nineveh. Not a token, not a reminiscence, of all the panting and perspiring thousands who all the week have run fiercely up and down this great stone cage, remains on wall or walk. The dens of the brokers—those spiders who weave their meshes of thin bank paper rags, even flimsier and more unsubstantial than the arachnean web—are all hermetically closed, as if they were the tombs of the victims who have there been slain and skinned. The "ponderous and marble jaws" of the innumerable banks are also shut tight—and, indeed, the whole street, on Sunday, looks not unlike a thickly populated avenue in some old cemetery, with the Custom House and the Exchange towering up like two gigantic mausolea, and the tall spire of Trinity springing like an exhalation into the sky, as if to point the way the souls of the departed ought to have taken.

But the churches, thickly planted like trees of promise in every quarter of the city, and the streets leading to them, present a totally different appearance. If, during the week, the stranger should be surprised at the intense activity and insane eagerness to make money which prevail among our business men, let him look at their handsome wives and daughters as they sail out to church in full Sunday apparel, and he will wonder no longer. This vast, uninterrupted stream of twenty-five dollar bonnets, fifty dollar silks, yard wide ribbons, embroidered shawls, velvet robes, and costly feathers, bespeaks an unparalleled extravagance in the families of the industrious and prosperous many who make up the great body of the population of every large city. The expensive and ostentatious style of this immense class, both in their dress and manner of living, is one of the most striking characteristics of our country and our age. Nowhere else in the world can one tenth part of so great a number of expensively (we do not say well) dressed women be seen in the same time or compass, as in Broadway on a fine Sunday morning. When we encountered this brilliant procession, last Sunday, and remembered that money was worth two per cent. a month in Wall street, we could not help roughly estimating the enormous interest the husbands and fathers of New York bestow upon their wives and daughters.

Sunday evening is given up to the denizens of the kitchen and steward's room. From dark till late into the night, the streets are filled with ruddy-cheeked and strong-armed chambermaids and house-servants, each with her "cousin," or "frind jist come over from the ould country," pacing proudly by her side. The habits of the drawing-room inevitably find their way into the lower departments of life, and the throng on Sunday evening is even more gaudily bedizened than its forerunner of the morning. It is, also, doubtless, far happier and more contented; for the study of life in a great city indelibly fixes this lesson deeply in the judgment—mankind are happy in an inverse ratio to their capacity of enjoyment.

II.

Rural Sights and Sounds in Dutchess County.

WASSAIC HOUSE, WASSAIC, July 4, 1853.

I AM happy to escape the "glorious Fourth" in New York, and not be half crazed by the tumult of the city. Rest, silence, and the majesty of mountains, all about and towering above me! What a contrast to the clatter, the dust and fiery rush of Broadway, with its two inch layer of dirt strewing the trampled sidewalk, and its hundreds of countermarching processions hurrying, driving, crushing madly through the streets! Nothing strikes my ear now save the tender whispering of the young leaves and the running brook that leaps joyfully at my feet. I have just come in from a ramble, and certainly never have I visited more admirably sited hills and mountains. They are spurs of the Green Mountains of Massachusetts and Vermont, running along the whole eastern boundary of Dutchess county and crossing to the Highlands. From one point, overlooking the city of Hudson and Poughkeepsie, can be seen distinctly in the distance the Cattskill Mountains. The grand far-sweeping landscape, together with the broad, majestic Hudson, lying thus in mysterious beauty beneath the soft blue light, seems like a great young heart, full of romantic dreams and glorious aspirations, on which the moonlight of first love is streaming. What of reality is yet crude and imperfect, sinks in the distance beneath the soft light, like the rocks and rugged monsters of the deep beneath the immortal grace of its undulating surface. Nothing but the vast line of beauty that pervades all nature, everywhere inclosing and marking out the ideal, is visible. All around, and in my own heart, is the peace, the serenity, the solemn splendor, of untamed, unmasked, unmaddened nature.

You will doubtless accuse me of extravagance in these expressions; but if you could stand with me amid the romantic and picturesque scenery I have been describing, or climb with me the green hills, turbaned with still greener forests, you would condemn my page as weak and feeble to describe what we were enjoying. I have never seen wild mountain scenery more happily blended.

The annual emigration from the metropolis to

the innumerable watering places, so called, spread over the face of the country and all along shore, is one of the most curious, comical, characteristic, and altogether remarkable phenomena which the society of the New World has produced. Of late years, the custom, like all other metropolitan fashions, has been imitated in a small way by other cities on the Atlantic coast, whose convulsive efforts at establishing grand-sounding "watering-places" are as ludicrous as their comforts and conveniences are pitiable. The good old-fashioned quietude and refreshing serenity of many small and pleasant places, situated in shady portions of the country, lying at convenient distances from the metropolis, are overlooked and forgotten in the spasmodic efforts to make a conspicuous display at a petty watering place. Here, in this shady retreat, we find rest and repose—inhale a pure, life-giving atmosphere from the mountains, without the great struggle for preëminence, the pleasureless and exhausting dissipations which reign at our summer watering places.

The Wassaic House is new, and well conducted by Mr. Atkins and his amiable wife, who take great pains to render the stay of their guests in every way pleasant. The rooms are large, well- ventilated and furnished, and we take pleasure in recommending the house to all those who wish quiet and substantial comfort at a moderate expense. It is on the Harlem railroad, which brings you here in two hours from New York, and is just the place in which to spend the summer months happily and contentedly.

The Harlem, by the way, is one of the best managed roads in the United States, and has had fewer accidents than many others. The conductors are polite, gentlemanly men, who always study the comfort and safety of their passengers. It is the pleasantest as well as the safest route to go anywhere north, either to Lebanon or Saratoga Springs.

III.

Annual Exhibition of the Amenia Seminary.—Pleasures of Rural Life.

WASSAIC HOUSE, WASSAIC, July 23, 1853.

ON Wednesday came off the annual exhibition of the Amenia Seminary—three miles from here. It is a Methodist institution, but, I understand, not a sectarian one. John W. Beech is the principal, and also a Methodist clergyman, who holds service every Sunday afternoon in the chapel connected with the seminary. He is young, possesses an interesting face, and, from appearance, I should suppose him a man of much intellect. The seminary consists of three buildings, beautifully located upon a gentle eminence, and surrounded by prettily laid out grounds, ornamented with flowers and fine old shade trees. The institution is in a flourishing condition, averaging from one hundred and twenty to one hundred and fifty pupils. The examination did much credit to the school; the compositions were good, and one of the dialogues was full of animation and evinced considerable talent. The only thing that did not please us was the elocution. The modulation was very imperfect. Whenever one speaks or writes, he is supposed, as a rational being, to have some end in view, either to inform, or to amuse, or to persuade, or in some way or other to influence his fellow-creatures. Reading without modulation, no effect can be produced. At the exhibition we observed that the reading was too much on one key, and that often pitched too high. Young speakers are apt to think more of what they say than how they say it—which is a fault. Any composition, however good, if not artistically read, loses half its force and meaning, and is discordant to the ear. Transition is as essential in speaking as in singing. The passing from one subject to another in reading is the same as a change of key in music, and should be studied and taught with as much care. Pleasing ideas can hardly be transmitted to the mind by means of harsh and disagreeable sounds.

At the present day, nothing is more needed than a practical treatise upon the voice, which is susceptible of a high state of cultivation in speaking as in singing. If some learned professor would accomplish the task, he would distinguish himself as the founder of eloquence, and confer a blessing upon mankind.

Dr. Rush, of Philadelphia, has written and published a most scientific work upon the voicc; but it is not a practical one. The method is nearly the same as that of music, and can only be applied by a thorough musician.

All is as still as Sunday morning number one in Eden, and while the citizens I have left behind are languid and suffocated with heat reflected from brick wall and pavement, here I sit absolutely filled with silence, and the sense of absolute repose and quiet, in a cool, delicious atmosphere, looking out of the window of my little room upon a green valley, dotted over with still greener hills, and watching the soft white clouds upon the blue sky, that ever and anon cast their shadows as if to make the picture more fresh and beautiful.

In the leafy months, the season of birds and flowers, I would wish to see all, weary and worn by metropolitan life, escape to quiet retreats and recover under their balmy and invigorating influence. I have just returned from the city, where I passed two or three days, and never before have I felt all the advantages of a summer country life, where we are not exposed incessantly to noxious exhalations, impure air, and extreme heat.

At this moment our beautiful valley is perfectly lighted up by the full moon, whose orbed sphere, air-poised above a coliseum of terraced mountains, flushed and palpitating with all unimaginable riches of light and shade, seems descending slowly to the lovely earth, drawn by some sweet and irresistible attraction—the orbs of heaven, the silence, the shadows, are steeped in poetry. Where moonlight falls, what heart would not be softened, and mind elevated, amid the loveliness of night's deepest and stillest hours?

We are getting on charmingly here. New arrivals every day. To-night we have a soirée, and our little folks are getting up a grand hop for next week, under the inspection of mamma and papa, and expect all the gay ones of the neighborhood to assist.

You can see by the busy and contented appearance of Mr. Atkins, as he hastens from parlor to parlor, and over his establishment, listening as if by instinct, and giving his orders with promptness and decision, that the season has fairly commenced, and a golden time in perspective. The scene is a fitting contrast to the solemnity and beauty without, and eye and heart turn from one to the other with a delicious alternation of sweet content.

IV.

Visit of Rev. Dr. Wainwright.—Rev. Mr. Frissell.—The Old Stone Church at Dover.—A Charade.

WASSAIC, WASSAIC HOUSE, August 5, 1853.

WE have been favored with the company of Dr. Wainwright, the right reverend bishop of the diocese. He made this picturesque spot his resting place while engaged in some of his diocesan visitations in this region of country. He expressed himself highly delighted with the union of fertility and beauty for which this section of eastern Dutchess has been so long and justly distinguished—a much more picturesque spot than strangers have any idea of from merely passing through it. The Wassaic Creek is small, but a beautiful stream, thickly wooded, and of charmingly variegated and undulating outline, here and there broken by golden fields of wheat, or a vista between the forest hill, where the still more golden light streams through.

Last Sunday, heard a good sermon from the

Rev. Mr. Frissell, the Presbyterian clergyman at South Amenia, where most of the inmates of the Wassaic House attend church. Mr. Frissel has a fine person, an impressive but pleasing presence, a good voice, which he uses artistically, and is an eloquent preacher. This field of public speaking has its advantages and disadvantages. It has some advantages peculiar to itself. The dignity and importance of its subject must be acknowledged superior to any other. But there are peculiar difficulties that attend the eloquence of the pulpit. His subjects of discourse are, in themselves, noble and important; but they are subjects trite and familiar. They have, for ages, employed so many speakers and so many pens; the public ear is so much accustomed to them that it requires more than an ordinary power of genius to fix attention. Nothing is more difficult in art than to bestow on what is common the grace of novelty. The merit of it lies wholly in the execution; not in giving any information that is new, not in convincing men of what they do not believe, but in dressing truths which they know, and of which they were before convinced, in such colors as most forcibly affect their imaginations and hearts.

The end of all preaching is to persuade men to become good. Every sermon, therefore, should be a persuasive oration. The chief characteristics of the eloquence suited to the pulpit, distinguished from other kinds of public speaking, are gravity and warmth. In the Rev. Mr. Frissel, it seems to me that these two most important characteristics are happily united, forming that character of preaching which the French call unction, the affecting, penetrating, interesting manner, flowing from a strong sensibility of heart in the preacher, to the importance of those truths which he delivers, and an earnest desire that they may make a full impression on the hearts of his hearers.

I have paid a visit to what is called the "old stone church" at Dover. It is not an antiquated church (as the name would signify), formed by human hands, and fallen to decay; but a phenomenon of nature. Our drive was a charming one—following the creek and winding among hills that seem nature's favored children; anon coming to neat-looking farm houses, nestled so securely as if to distract the mind for a moment from the beautiful landscapes of nature seen on every side.

The place of destination was reached at last, and

the rewarding sight awaited us. I was led into church, not to listen to a sermon, but the sound of many waters. The rock which forms this curious phenomenon in nature is a hundred and fifty or two hundred feet in height, the aperture from fifty to seventy-five feet in width, and at the top almost as elaborately arched as if wrought by an architect. The water falls at the extreme end from seventy five to a hundred feet, but being broken in severa. places the height of the greatest fall is not more than forty feet.

It is not easy to describe in words the precise impression which grand and sublime objects make upon us when we behold them; but every one has a conception of it. It produces a sort of internal elevation and expansion; it raises the mind much above its ordinary state, and fills it with a degree of wonder, awe, and astonishment, which it can not express.

This wonder has long been visited by strangers, and will continue to be; and I would suggest that artificial steps be placed beside the falls, so that visitors may ascend to the top, and look down upon its excessive grandeur, which would heighten its sublimity.

The Wassaic House is fast filling up to overflowing, and our agreeable host, Mr. Atkins, is doing every thing that can be done in the way of drives and getting up amusements to make the time pass away pleasantly; for which we propose a vote of thanks. His table is excellent and abundant, and all those who give him a call will be sure to come again. Among the recent arrivals, we have Hamilton Robinson, Esq., and family, of New York; William B. Torrey, Esq., and family, of Brooklyn, whose pretty and accomplished wife does much in aiding and directing our amusements, being one of the finest musicians in this country; Mrs. Hall and daughters, and Miss Lyne, of Brooklyn; Miss Patterson and brother, Philadelphia; Mr. Talmage Patterson, and Adriance Talmage, New York.

This evening we have had a charade—the word selected was courtship. The first scene was a representation of Queen Victoria's drawing room. The next scene, a ship bound for California, named Wassaic. The closing scene, Yankee courtship. The whole passed off with éclat, and did much credit to those engaged in it. Queen Victoria, Miss Patterson, attired in white robe and train, ornamented with white flowers. Princess Adelaide of Hoenlohe, Miss M. Andrews, New York; dress, blue brocade and train. Duchess of Kent, Miss A. Heath, New York; dress, green and crimson brocade. Duchess of Sutherland, Miss Talmage, Brooklyn; dress, green tissue. Duchess of Buckingham, Miss Foster, New York; dress, blue glace silk and train. Duchess of Cumberland, Miss M. Heath, New York; dress, pink silk, trimmed with black lace. Lady Flora Hastings, Miss E. Heath, New York; dress, blue silk. Prince Albert, E. Patterson, New York. Prince of Wales, Master Torrey, Brooklyn. Lord Chamberlain, A. Talmage, New York. Duke of Cumberland, T. Patterson, New York.

After the charade, the folding doors were thrown open, and supper announced, provided by Mr. Atkins in his best style, and gave great satisfaction to all. The company was ushered in by the Grand Master of Ceremonies, G. Andrews, Esq., of New York. At supper, the health of the Queen was drank and that of Prince Albert. The health of N. Gridley, Esq., was proposed, owner of the Wassaic House, to which he responded. He rose and said: "I feel highly complimented with the courtesy paid me this evening, and not the less so coming from royal lips. In our democratic country, court scenes are but seldom represented, and especially in this quiet and primitive section; but I assure this royal assembly of beauty and talent that the novelty is eminently appreciated and very acceptable." (Applause.)

The health of Mr. and Mrs. Atkins was proposed. Mr. Atkins rose and said: "I am truly gratified to find that I am favored with guests possessing merit and genius of no common order; and to those ladies and gentlemen who have been kind enough to offer this amusement for the benefit of the company, sincere gratitude." (Applause.)

The company retired, much gratified with the entertainment, amidst music and applause.

V.

The Warm Weather.—An Amusing Incident.—The Beautiful Evening.

WASSAIC, WASSAIC HOUSE, August 22, 1853.

THANKS to the attractions and hospitalities of the Wassaic House that I was not in that salamander safe, New York, to be parboiled and suffocated by the unusual and terrific heat which visited the city last week. The number of deaths from *coup de soliel* was truly lamentable. The poor laborers—the bone and sinew of the community—whose days and hours are not all their own, who seldom, if ever, inhale a breath of untainted air; but toil, with hod on shoulder filled with brick and mortar, for a scanty sustenance—climbing the ladder to the topmost story of buildings for the rich who know no want—exposed to rays of heat that are so soon to consume the poor man's life, leaving dependent his already ill clad and fed family in despair. What a picture! Could not the rich builder give the employée a few hours' recess in the middle of the day in extreme hot weather without curtailing his wages, which he can not afford to dispense with? That would be humane and charitable, and save many lives and much misery, and make the employer happier if not richer for the good he had done.

The only exciting event we have had this week was on the occasion of the nervous lady declaring, in a fit of dyspepsia, that she must have a drive. The gallant Mr. P., of Philadelphia, who, by the way, is a great favorite, being over-civil and complimentary to the ladies, immediately proclaimed if there was a vehicle to be had, it would give him great pleasure to accompany her; to which she smiled, simpered and bowed her thanks. Mr. P. repaired to Mr. Atkins, but returned in a few minutes, with feigned disappointment depicted in every feature, saying that every mode of conveyance was out, and that they would be under the necessity of waiting for the express train cars, which would convey them to any point between that and Albany. The lady indignantly declared that she could not bear the horrid cars; that her health was so delicate—at the same moment assuming a sweet smile, looking at Mr. P., saying, in the blandest tone, that nothing but a drive and his agreeable company would restore her. Mr. P., like all very young and very old gentlemen, quite attentive, went out to explore, and after a two hours' search, returned with a horse and wagon. The nag was rather long and slender—something of the eel style, and traveled very much as an eel swims. The wagon was in keeping, with a very long, narrow box, the seat quite in front, barely room for the feet a little cramped. The buffalo robe was placed upon the seat; madam assisted in, Mr. P. seating himself on her right; she being in a charming sweet temper, invited Master A. to take a drive with them. He accepted; but there being no seat for him, she ordered a chair. It was brought and placed in the back of the wagon. Master A. took his seat, looking like a living statue, upon a very high pedestal clinging for support. They drove off amid good wishes and the waving of handkerchiefs. The road being good, all passed pleasantly, with the single exception of the horse being a little restive, which was the subject of many amusing remarks. After an hour's drive, the lady forgot her age and dyspepsia, and chatted, lisped, and smiled, expressing

herself most extravagantly about the scenery, saying that was sublime and compared with the Alps, the other was grand and reminded her of the Rhine—that was beautiful and very much like her own little town. Mr. P. was unusually brilliant and witty, quoting from Shakespeare and Byron. Master A. listened with much attention, remarking occasionally that his seat was too high, and that he felt a little wearied with his long reach, clinging to the back of the seat.

All things combined, the drive seemed to promise to be a green spot in their memories. "But a change came o'er the spirit of their dreams." Just as they were on the borders of Connecticut, and ascended a hill, the horse sheered off, and, at the same time, giving a spring, and a very comical twist of the body, Master A., chair and all, were sent over the back of the wagon, he alighting directly on the top of his head. Madam, witnessing the accident, modulated from the sweetest of lisps to the most unearthly of screeches, much to the alarm of a gentleman who was riding a few rods forward of them, but not seeing the accident supposed the lady to be in hysterics. He was soon by her side. Discovering the cause of alarm, he raised

Master A., who looked a little pale and somewhat dusty, the lady reiterating the whole time that his neck was broken, notwithstanding he held up his head as straight as a corporal in a June training. After the nerves of the lady were a little composed, and Master A. had given several turns of the head to reassure all that his neck was yet sound, he was put into the seat between madam and Mr. P., who resumed the ribbons, humming, by the way, airs from "Robert le Diable." Master A. uttered a few groans, saying he wished he had stayed at home. Madam sighed; but all arrived, without further accident, in time for tea, when mirth and sadness, heads and hearts, were forgotten over a cup of Mrs. Atkins's best black tea.

Yesterday we had one of the heaviest showers, accompanied by thunder and lightning, I have ever witnessed, which, by the way, has been an almost daily occurrence this week, much to the discomfiture of several parties who had gone out for a drive. About one o'clock this morning the wind changed to the north, and the rest of the night it howled a most mournful dirge as if singing the requiem of the departed summer. From the atmosphere now it seems it was not all in vain, for the soul of summer has departed, and to-day we are shivering in our shawls.

Last night, soon after the shower, the fair, chaste moon, just rounding into the full outline of her most dazzling beauty, drawing with silver fingers the filmy tracery of the clouds about her as a robe of loveliness, darted the radiance of her smiles upon them until they beamed with all the separate yet harmonious colorings of crystallized light. It was like the dreams of youth painted by the prism of hope. All over the eastern heavens sailed graceful clouds of orange and silver, like troops of spirits bearing gigantic wreaths where-with to crown their bride-mistress, while the bright goddess herself, flushed as when she stooped to kiss Endymion, swam amid a celestial halo of many-colored splendors. The thousands of admiring and rapt faces which had been mutely upturned to heaven to witness the magnificent scene, sought their pillows and their dreams—and the noiseless universe went on its way.

VI.

Life at Watering Places.—The Pequot House.—Our Boarders.

PEQUOT HOUSE, NEW LONDON, August 28, 1854.

THE philosophy of life at a fashionable watering place is something not yet much studied not properly understood in our democratic country. It is here that the reverse of the medal of life appears; and instead of every thing being controlled by man, the entire government of the affairs of the community is in the hands of the women. The prettiest and boldest woman is Sultana, whose lightest smile and faintest nod is unquestioned and irresistible law; while those of less means and fewer attractions, are Mayor, Aldermen and Common Council, who pass their time in eating, sleeping, dressing and undressing, and are continually hard at work trying to be idle with a good grace. In such a government as this men are nobodies; the muslins and laces of Stewart's, so beautifully transparent; are emblazonry of the royal standard, which every good citizen feels himself bound to honor, to uphold; coats are but quaint ornaments for the unconsidered.

In this brilliant little kingdom of New London, therefore, we have a fair opportunity of judging how far the "delicate creatures" are deserving of consideration in matters of government and State policy which a portion of the sex so pertinaciously claim. But, alas! the "good time coming," when women shall rule, and men roast, promises to be only a change instead of an amelioration. Our little oligarchy is already cut up into as many rival cliques and factions as the political parties of this country. I have come to the conclusion that it is injudicious for women to wish to wield the scepter, except in kingdoms like this. Let them be faithful and patriotic, without encroaching upon the province of the other sex—waste their time, and bore their friends by writing and lecturing upon the equality of the sexes, and what they call "woman's rights"—leave political and financial topics, State policy, and the struggle of war to abler heads, stronger arms, and sterner hearts.

The Pequot House has not been fuller, nor more fashionable this season, than at the present time. It will not close until the 1st of October. I understand a great dress ball is to come off next month. We have innumerable numbers of celebrities, great and small, of all ages, sizes, and conditions, continually arriving at and departing from this delightful place. Mr. Mather, our munificent landlord, has engaged for our pleasure and amusement two harpists and a violinist, who discourse most heart-stirring music in the hall during the hours of dinner and evening, embalming the atmosphere and all around with those charming airs, selected from the most popular operas, until the senses are bathed and heart rapt as in a delicious dream. There is something intoxicating and fascinating in the sound of music—the little ones skip about like inspired fairies, and old ones unconsciously look charming. It is truly the language of the heart. They played the finale of "Lucia" in a style to recall by-past days, when Benedetti sang and acted it, in such a manner as to hold his hearers breathless and spell-bound with delight. Poor Benedetti! that he should have lost the voice that would have charmed and astonished the world and made a fortune for himself.

At this moment I see from my window, on the balcony, Miss D——, of Norwich, looking very sweetly in that pink dress, and Mr. M——, of Middletown. I think there is no sentiment—they look too happy and too well satisfied with themselves for that. There goes the *distingué* Mr. H——, of New York, who was promenading last evening with the stylish and pleasing Miss C. P——, of New York. The Misses G——s, of New York, are very pretty girls, and dress in exquisite taste. Mrs. P——t, of New York, is an intelligent and charming woman, and her daughter a sweet and graceful girl. Miss H——, of East Haddam, is also very pretty. She has light and laughing eyes, sunny brown hair, and faultless mouth. Among the recent arrivals, I notice one very beautiful, Miss H——ff, of Middletown, daughter of Captain H——. Mr. J——, who has just returned from abroad, dances well, and would be quite fascinating if he did not embalm himself so sacredly in that comfortable looking gray coat of his. Pray omit it in the dance for a black one of less dimensions.

The first rain we have had here in a month fell last night; still the weather here has not been oppressive, but cool and delightful.

VII.

Notes of Notable People and Matters in Connecticut.

PEQUOT HOUSE, NEW LONDON, August 17, 1854.

How changed the whole scene since the young, ambitious Winthrop struggled through the wilderness from Saybrook, some two hundred years ago, in search of a place to found a town. How his heart would swell with delight if he could look down with earthly feelings and survey the fair spot and town that he hewed out and founded in the wilderness. The old town, burnt by Arnold, could boast of very little elegance; the houses were old, tottering on the verge of decay, and those that replaced them, built by an impoverished people, could not boast, with few exceptions, of elegance, taste, or neatness. The city now contains ten structures for public worship, two of them new and elegant, in the Gothic style of architecture; a custom house and county prison, both of granite; several manufacturing establishments, two of which employ

engines of great power and several hundred men; several blocks of stately brick buildings, in one of which is a spacious hall for public exhibitions; and many elegant private mansions.

John Winthrop, Jr., called the younger, the founder of New London, and chosen governor of the colony, was educated at the University of Dublin. In 1627, when twenty-one years of age, he was in the service of the unfortunate Duke of Buckingham, in the fruitless attempt to assist the Protestants of Rochelle, in France. John Winthrop, his father, was the leader of that second Puritan emigration from England which settled the colony of Massachusetts, and he was chosen governor of that colony. The family seat of the Winthrops in England was at Groton, in Suffolk. Hence the name Groton bestowed on those lands east of the river Thames, which were first included in New London, and where stands Groton Monument overlooking the harbor, and forming an impressive feature of the place. Under its shadow lie the ruins of old Fort Griswold, from whose battlements a fine view is obtained of the town and the river. From the summit of the monument, the prospect to the south of the Sound, its coasts and its islands, is absolutely peerless and magnificent. In the forefront of the town stands Fort Trumbull, a fine specimen of mural architecture, complete in design and finish, massive, new, and in perfect order.

Dear reader, have you ever visited this delightful of all delightful places of summer resort, the Pequot House? In wandering about the country, as I have done from Washington to the watering places, and wherever beauty and fashion most do congregate, I assure you I have never before seen such a blending of attraction, enjoyment, and comfort. The house is new and spacious, handsomely furnished, a fine dining saloon, tables profusely furnished with all the luxuries of the season, and served in perfect order and elegance. Mr. Mather, our landlord, and his clerk, Mr. Lyon, are well-bred, gentlemenly men, who anticipate the wants of their guests, and that is unusual in our democratic country. Another attractive feature is, the hotel has many attached cottages, beautifully fitted up, containing drawing rooms, a number of bed-chambers, and all the conveniences of a household, suitable for a family or a party. I have been here some time, and I have not yet heard the first murmur of dissatisfaction from a guest, but many eulogies upon the superior accommodations of the house. The bathing, walks, and drives, are fine; and lest I degenerate into an absolute puff, I will say no more, concluding by simply inviting you to call at the Pequot House, and see if I do not speak the truth, when I say it is unequaled, in all respects, by most of the watering places in the Union.

There has not as yet been any "reigning belle" of the present season elected. The honors seem to be pretty equally divided, although we have many pretty faces and some queenly beauties. Among the guests, we have the queenly and dignified Mrs. Daniel Webster, and her pretty friend, Miss Canon, who are located for the season. Jacob LeRoy and family, New York; and Hon. J. S. Wendell, Hon. J. Pringle Jones and family, Pennsylvania; Hon. H. J. Dickey and family, Chicago; Mayor Skinner, the munificent and popular municipal prince of New Haven. Their municipal affairs are something to deserve the name in such hands. He displays, in his manners and intercourse with others, all that suavity and polished dignity which constitute the high-bred gentleman.

Governor Dalton and family, New Haven; and Professor Bears, Rev. A. L. Stone, Boston; Rev. Dr. Broadhead, New York; Rev. R. W. Sealy, Springfield, Massachusetts; and many others equally distinguished.

Bowling is the fashionable anti-dyspeptic regimen at New London. I would suggest billiards, it being a more graceful game. However, bowling, and robes that sweep the alleys, and have consequently to be held daintily back with one hand, while the other launches the fatal ball upon its career, are all the rage. There are duller sights, I assure you, than an animated bowling match between such lustrous beauties as the spirituelle Mrs. L. R——, the queenly Mrs. J——, and the graceful Miss O——.

I look out of the window of my little dormitory upon a magnificent park. Along the walks leap groups of lovely and laughing children, arrayed in all a mother's pride condensed into the quaintest and most picturesque costumes that ever a fairy milliner imagined, while within the deep shade of the portico that lines the inner court of the beautiful domain, saunter, with maddening pace, the owners of magnetic eyes and graceful forms, superb in the air of indifference with which they accept the homage of the gentlemen who attend upon them as assiduously as a toady upon his patron, or a new author upon a literary big-bug. It is lull of the day—the interval between the morning walk and dinner—and the majority of the beautiful creatures, assembled in the great caravansera of fashionabledom, are deeply immersed in the occult mysteries of the toilet, although a few of the freshest and loveliest, with a beautiful disdain of all dress and preparation, to which, a few seasons hence, they will thankfully and reverently resort, have escaped betimes from their narrow bedroom, and hurried out for a walk and a rendezvous upon the balcony.

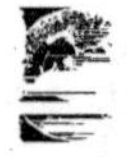

The after dinner drive is the pleasantest and most rational portion of the day, and is really in every way delightful and refreshing. Then come tea and tattle, and the grand military review and parade of the evening, when beauty's regiment, divided into squadrons and platoons, and officered by men in black, marches in sweeping pace up and down the long piazza. The hop ends the ostensible and regular performances of the day—which taper off into scandals and suppers, moonlight rambles and sofa lounges, until all subsides into midnight, and New London sleeps.

VIII.

The Sound.—The Aborigines.—Pleasure-Seekers.—Hon. John Cotton Smith.

PEQUOT HOUSE, NEW LONDON, September 14, 1857.

WHAT a lovely day! The air is spicy and fragrant as if a cool breeze from the Green Mountains had just been melted into it. The water is sparkling with sunbeams whose surface ever presents to the eye a changeful scene. Barges and boats whose oars dip liquid silver; the smack with its slant sheet bearing up before the wind; schooners built for use, and deep with freight, display only ease and grace in form and motion; lines of steamers, making neighborhood of distance, are objects which give a pleasing variety to the surface of the Sound, whose waters I am at this moment overlooking from my window.

I have just returned from a day's visit to the city, and never was Paradise more welcome to the weary feet of stumbling and travel-stained Christian pilgrim, than this lovely retreat to me. This month promises to be the most delightful one here. One can ramble in the beautiful groves and fields surrounding this place, and along shore, without an exuberance of heat, and drink in this invigorating atmosphere, insuring a full stock of health for opening the winter's campaign in the city, which can not be gained in warmer months. He can survey Connecticut and Long Island, for ever looking at each other from their pretty shores, bound in love, linked as they are by ties of common interest, and guarding with watchful care that inland sea which, won from the ocean, lies like a noble captive between them, reduced to their service, and enclosed by their protecting arms.

I often amuse myself, as I watch the sunset clouds hovering like vast flocks of birds over the distant hills, by drawing comparisons in my imagination between the scenes of three centuries ago, enacted around these forest-guarded waters, and those which at this hour pass before and around me. The belles of those times, as they sauntered about with their pretty legs encased in buckskin leggins, terminated by neat wampumed moccasins, and their swarthy shoulders exposed almost as low as the whiter and thinner ones of their Anglo-Saxon successors; or squatted on the greensward, with their brawny lovers, beside the water, cut rather a different figure from the fair and dashing daughters of the New York aristocracy who promenade the broad portico of the Pequot House, swathed in clouds of diaphanous muslins and brocade silks, their pale cheeks glowing with an effulgence, and their mincing feet encased in the daintiest of kid slippers. And the beaux—what a contrast! Figure to yourself a herculean Pequot warrior, his immense shoulders and muscular legs bare, his face and breast beautifully tattooed in red ochre and blue paint, and his head surmounted by a crescent of bright-colored feathers—his blanket carelessly thrown around him, and a tomahawk and its twin scalping-knife ostentatiously displayed in his wampum belt, strutting about with the air of a king; and then compare him with the lankey and attenuated dandies of the present day, in tight coat and checked trowsers, who usurp the favorite walks of the red man, and dawdle around his most sacred haunts. Could the spirits of Sassacus and Uncas return to this spot as it now appears, what would be their "first impressions" of all they would see and hear? Would they prefer a bath to the high rock?

a drive to a sail in the light canoe? settle their old differences and drink each other's healths in a bottle of sparkling champagne? music and the hop to the whoop and the war dance?

In looking over this lovely place, one can scarcely realize that it is the identical spot where once was enacted that terrible scene, the most atrocious and unrelenting of wars, the Pequot—now the resort ot so much of fashion and gayety. It is sad to think that these pure waters have closed over the fate ot those children of the forest, dispatched by Captain Stoughton's company, a little without the harbor. The object of Stoughton's expeditions from Massachusetts was to extirpate, if possible, the remaining Pequots. The English forces, guided by Indian allies, Mohegans and Narragansetts, who knew every pass of the country, were successful.

We are getting on famously here. Every day brings some new pleasure-seekers, and we still retain, spell-bound and charmed, many of our most pleasing guests. The stylish Miss P——, of New York; the amiable Miss L——, of Norwich; the agreeable Miss L—— R——, of New York; Hon. Samuel Williston, East Hampton; Thurlow Weed and family, Albany, and many others equally distinguished and interesting. Let us stop a moment, however, by this window, and observe that fine-looking man of thirty-six or eight, with Roman profile and true Anglo-Saxon head—who is he? That is Hon. John Cotton Smith, of Connecticut, and, they say, prospective Governor. He belongs to one of the oldest and most respectable families in the country, has a noble and commanding presence, a handsome and pleasing face, most *distingué* air and manner, and as a matter of course attracts many a glance from the fair sex. He lived abroad some years, and there associated with the highest and most refined circles. He possesses all the truthfulness and frankness of a New England gentleman, blended with the cultivation and fascination of a high-bred foreigner.

Mr. Mather's exertions to please and make comfortable his guests, are in no way diminished as the season draws to a close, and the company seem to fully appreciate his efforts. No doubt those who come here next season will be legion, and meet many familiar faces. I understand they design making new improvements, and building large additions to this already fine establishment. The house will be kept open until about the 1st of October.

I have just come in from a promenade on the balcony. It is perfectly lighted by the full moon, whose orbed sphere, air-poised between sky and wave, flushed and palpitating with all unimaginable riches of light and shade, seems descending slowly to the lovely earth, drawn by some sweet and irresistible attraction.

IX.

Leave-Taking.—Revolutionary Reminiscences.—Fashion and Display.—The Norwich Steamers.

PIQUOT HOUSE, NEW LONDON, September 18, 1854.

LEAVE-TAKING has already commenced, but not without many regrets that this brilliant little kingdom of the "Pequot" must be interrupted for a brief season. King, prince, and clerk of the metropolis must all return to the city, get ready for the coming election, look after the stocks, and resume money making, which is quite as necessary as spending it, in this hard-working, close-calculating country. The queen, and her maids of honor too, must leave the sounding sea, the quietude and refreshing serenity, sacred haunts of contemplation and repose, to the dryads and naiads of stream and forest, and return to their palatial homes in Fifth Avenue and Union Square, to inspect the fruit, look after the sweetmeats and hearts, exhaust all the scandal of the town, get ready for the opera, find out where they can buy the handsomest and most expensive dresses, the richest laces, adopt the fall fashions, and live in a perfect turmoil of excitement to excel their aristocratic neighbors.

The parting, however, of the guests does not resemble the flight of the inhabitants at the storming of Fort Griswold by traitor Arnold, although we have had some sharp shooting and many hearts taken captive, but no instance of a heart being pierced through with its own arrow after a surrender. The pleasant and agreeable circle must part with the sweet promise on their lips, the bright hope in the heart, of returning with the early birds and flowers—when there will be a reunion of hearts, and renewal of friendships, of cherished and pleasant remembrances; to walk or drive on the beach; to climb to the top of the light-house, or sit on the high rock and overlook the Sound, with its myriads of sails, and scan in the distance Groton monument, a fine specimen of architecture, reared to mark the spot of the closing scene of that most awful tragedy, the storming of Fort Griswold. How General Arnold could find it in his heart to steal upon his own people and kin (his birth-place being at Norwich, twelve miles distant from New

London,) under cover of night, and commit such butcheries, is a problem too difficult to solve. Our Puritan forefathers came to this countay for "conscience' sake," but seem to have had very little left after their arrival; and occasionally, to this day, we meet faces among their descendants possessing, in expression, their Christian sternness.

When the fort surrendered, few of the garrison had fallen. At least three fourths of the killed were sacrificed after the surrender. When the gate was opened, the enemy marched in, firing upon the retreating party. The British officer, at the head of the division, cried out, "Who commands this fort?" "I did, sir, but you do now," replied Colonel Ledyard, raising and lowering his sword in token of submission, and advancing to present it to him The ferocious officer received the sword and plunged it up to the hilt in the owner's bosom, while his attendants, rushing upon the falling hero, dispatched him with their bayonets. The American army at this time was small. Youths were put on duty; commanders left their vessels in the harbor and fought in this battle. Daniel Williams, of Saybrook, was, perhaps, the youngest. His tombstone bears this inscription: "Fell in the action at Fort

Griswold, on Groton Hill, in the fifteenth year of his age." Thomas, son of Lieutenant Parke Avery, aged seventeen, was killed fighting by the side of his father. As he fell, "'Tis in a good cause," said the father, and remained firm at his post. Such was the struggle for freedom in this beautiful country.

Notwithstanding the lateness of the season, we daily have some new arrivals; and our kind host shows the same solicitude for their comfort and convenience as two months since. A number of the guests have already engaged rooms for next season, and hope to find Mr. Mather at his post.

The display and ostentation at our fashionable watering-places, like every thing else permitted by divine wisdom, have their uses. They serve especially to set afloat and restore to the circulating medium of the country, the hoarded thousands gained by stingy intrigue or dishonest speculation during the other months of the year. The summer emigration from the metropolis is fast growing of a more important and noticeable character. The numerous and rapidly-increasing class of our really wealthy families—the strong infusion of foreign manners and languages, are fast communicating to

it a homogeneous character, forming the substratum of a real aristocracy, composed of the three elements of wealth, intelligence, and *ton*, which, in a few years, will crystallize into a veritable, respectable, and self-sustaining aristocracy. We do not look with the distrust entertained or affected by many, upon this natural, rational and interesting development of republican society. The object and effect of republican institutions is not to destroy these social distinctions, the germs of which have been planted by the Creator himself, but to substitute for the false and oppressive systems, created by the antiquity of family and law of primogeniture, elements of real social distinction, founded upon energy of character, moral worth, intellectual greatness, and eminence of distinguished services or achievements. To this kind of aristocracy all must bow, for it is patented and authorized by the law of nature and the law of God. And such an aristocracy we must enevitably have in New York; but the preliminary movements and notions in the process of its formation will necessarily be curious and interesting enough.

If you would get here quickly, and without loss of time or sleep, I would advise you to take the new and elegant steamboats Knickerbocker, or Connecticut. They leave pier No. 18, North River, foot of Courtlandt street, every afternoon. Their accommodations are fine, tables excellent; and we take pleasure in commending them to the traveling public, as being the best route from New York to New London, Norwich, Worcester, and Boston.

The guests of the Pequot were agreeably surprised last evening by a serenade given by the New London brass band. The delicious music embalmed the midnight air as with voices of dreams. As the stream of sound gathered strength, and swept on upon the awakened breeze, they sighed to find themselves awakening too, lest the blissful music of their dreams should fade into silence. We take pleasure in chronicling so pleasing an incident in the harmonious history of the Pequot, and cheerfully add that nothing was ever better timed.

X.

Niagara Falls.—The Suspension Bridge.—The Luna Bow. —The Clifton House.

Cataract House, Niagara Falls, November 5, 1854.

As I took my seat at Albany in one of those elegant and comfortable cars of the New York Central Railroad, for a first visit to the Falls, I felt a breathless anxiety not to be disappointed in viewing, for the first time, the most sublime and interesting wonder of the globe. As I passed up the valley of the Mohawk, a beautiful tract of fertile soil, adorned with the richest vegetation, and watered by sparkling streams—those blue veins of the globe which circulate life and vigor through its system—I felt my mind expanding, and preparing for the effect of nature's greatest wonder.

The New York Central Railroad is built in the most substantial manner, and is managed with great ability and energy. Its conductors are obliging and courteous men. The fine scenery, the many beautiful old towns and villages it passes through, makes it a most pleasant route, though the points of interest are not of a striking nature.

As you approach Niagara, and listen, for the first time, to the ceaseless roar of the cataract, the mind is filled with emotions of awe, grandeur, and sublimity which it is perfectly impossible to describe. I am convinced that no description by the pen can ever give the least idea of the cataract. It must be seen and felt before its grandeur and immense sublimity can be appreciated. But there is a work of art within sight, of majestic greatness, which, for beauty of proportion, and strength and elegance of construction, can almost vie with the master-piece of nature. The Railroad Suspension Bridge, spanning the mighty stream below "the Falls," is one of the most interesting structures of human genius. So lofty, it seems to float in the air, yet firm as if its whole course were based upon the solid earth. A second track, above the present way, is preparing for the railroad trains, and by the 1st of March will be completed; and unless unforeseen difficulties arise, the first railway train will pass over; and then will be seen in its full extent the triumph of art applied to public utility.

I know of nothing on the continent of America which approaches this work in beauty, grandeur and greatness of design. It must be a gigantic genius to devise a bridge which should give safe passage to hundreds of tons of weight by a suspension of iron cords from abutment to abutment. It is already looked upon with as much interest by the tourist as the Falls themselves. This bridge connects the New York Central road with the Great Western Railway. The interest at the Falls, in connection with the bridge—the greatest iron bridge in the world—is an inducement for travelers to come this route. The Great Western or Canada road was opened in February last. I am told that no expense has been spared to make it perfect. The amount of travel by this route is already immense, and is the best evidence of its popularity. There are nearer, but no better, points at Niagara to get a full view of the Falls, than crossing this bridge. Passengers, by coming this route, may see the Falls without loss of time or additional expense.

I would advise tourists to visit the Falls when the moon is within two or three days previous or after its full, as it is the only time when the Luna Bow can be seen. When the weather is clear, fre-

quently a whole arch can be seen, with three colors, very distinct, and, I believe, is the only place on the globe where a rainbow at night, in the form of an arch, can be seen at all. It is indescribably grand, worthy the attention of the tourist, and will amply pay him for a trip to the Falls. Travelers coming this route, whose time is limited, would do well to go to the Clifton House, on the Canada side, to pass the night. It is a fine, large hotel, surrounded by beautiful pleasure grounds. In doing so, they will have ample time to see the Falls before the morning train leaves, and can also have a fine view of the Falls at sunrise, without leaving the house. This view is unsurpassed, and has no rival in grandeur, sublimity and interest.

XI.

Growth of Illinois.—Michigan Central Railroad.—The Chicago Breakwater.—The Tremont House.—Emigration.

TREMONT HOUSE, CHICAGO, November 7, 1854.

I WOULD like to give your readers some of the facts in regard to the growth of this city and State—its railroad communication, the which would become more interesting, and, I might add, more astonishing than the wildest visions of the most vagrant imagination. It is but thirty-six years since the State government of Illinois was formed, a State which has now more than a million of inhabitants, and whose principal commercial city has more than sixty thousand people, three thousand miles of railroad finished and in operation, and a year from now another thousand will be added. On these rails there are daily leaving and entering the city forty-six trains, making in all ninety-two trains per day, entering here, to accommodate travelers and commerce. Another important fact, in speaking of Chicago, as a great railroad center. All her roads have been projected and will be built by private enterprise. This shows that capitalists have placed abundant confidence in her commercial position. Eastern capitalists have been astonished at the low prices of railroad stock at the central States, who are ignorant of their resources, and the cheapness with which roads are built, not costing one half to build them in prairie States as it does in an eastern one. A fact worth repeating, that Chicago has three thousand miles of railroad in operation centering in it, and does not owe a single dollar for their construction.

At the session of the Legislature in 1836–'7, the State entered upon a splendid scheme of "internal improvement." Some thirteen hundred miles of railroad to be at once completed, and five millions of dollars were expended in locating and grading them. A general financial embarrassment followed those years of madness and folly, the credit of the State went down, and bankruptcy and a general suspension of the public works were the consequence. In 1841 the total State indebtedness amounted to fifteen millions of dollars. The only mistake the statesmen of that period made, their plans were in advance of the times they lived in. Twenty years will accomplish, by private enterprise, for the State of Illinois, much more than the statesmen of '36–'37 expected to realize. Chicago's railroad and water communication has given an impetus to its commerce and prosperity, and the Garden City has more than trebled her population in the short space of six years.

There is no more pleasant route in the Union than the "Michigan Central," from Detroit to this city. It is unequaled for speed, comfort and safety. Its cars are new and elegant—its conductors polite and obliging, and its careful and successful management renders it worthy of an immense patronage. It passes through Ann Arbor, the location of the Michigan University, a beautiful town, and Jackson, the location of the Penitentiary. At Marshall is the central dining establishment, almost enclosed by parks, filled with beautiful shade trees, and is unequaled by any eastern depot. The machine shops at Marshall are worthy a notice. They keep sixteen to twenty locomotives in order, to run one division of the road—making three divisions from Detroit to this city, a distance of two hundred and sixty-four miles.

In all, twenty-four locomotives, mostly built in Detroit, and some of the finest I have ever seen. The engine house has twenty-three stalls, built in a circle of about two hundred feet in diameter, and takes in half the circle. In the center is a turn-table to turn every engine into a stall. Machines suitable for making and repairing locomotives. I was shown locomotives that would run one hundred and twenty miles in three hours and a half, and make from sixteen to twenty stops, to take on and leave passengers. On this road pass eighteen to twenty long passenger cars, well filled, and from a hundred and thirty to a hundred and fifty, loaded with merchandise, passing east and west every day.

The breakwater opposite this city is a very expensive and difficult work. It extends nearly two miles, and will cost, when completed, seven hundred and fifty thousand dollars. For a mile it is built in the Lake, the inside line being four hundred feet from the east side of Michigan avenue. The Michigan and Illinois Central railroads both enter the city upon this track. This great work commences at the South Pier. From the pier to the engine house the breakwater is twelve feet wide. The area enclosed and reserved from the dominion of the Lake is about thirty-three acres. Upon this area the Illinois and Michigan railroads are erecting first, one passenger station-house, four hundred and fifty feet long by one hundred and sixty-five wide, including a car shed. The north-west corner of this building will be occupied exclusively for office and passenger rooms, and will be forty by one hundred and twenty feet, and three stories high. A freight building, six hundred by one hundred feet; grain house one hundred by two hundred, and one hundred feet high, to the top of the elevators, calculated to hold five hundred thousand bushels. Three tracks will run into the freight house, eight tracks into the passenger house, and two tracks into the grain house. The basin lying between the freight and grain houses will be five hundred by one hundred and seventy-eight feet, and will open into the river. All these buildings are to be constructed of stone obtained from Joliet. The cost of the buildings is not far from two hundred and fifty thousand dollars. The whole work will be finished this year.

Chicago is not as unhealthy as has been supposed. It is constantly fanned by pure breezes from the Lake, sweeping over hundreds of miles; with an efficient system of sewerage from lake to river, and stone pavement, I know no reason why it should not become as healthy as any eastern city. At present Chicago is paved with oak plank, and almost every outlet leading from it. Planks make a fine carriage-way, and never shall I forget my pleasant drives at Chicago.

I must not close without a well merited eulogy upon the Tremont House, kept by Gage and Brother, of Boston, who leased and opened in 1849. It was then predicted a bad speculation. They have from its profits already realized a handsome fortune. The house contains two hundred rooms, and will accommodate three hundred guests. The average arrivals per day are three hundred. It is built, finished and furnished equal to any in New York. I take much pleasure in commending it to all who visit Chicago. I have never seen better attendance or more profusely set tables. The house, notwithstanding its great transient patronage, is perfectly quiet—conducted with a system our eastern landlords might study with profit. Mr. Gage is a pleasing, gentlemanly man, and seeks to make all his guests comfortable.

The position of Chicago is not less favorable for

a manufacturing town than a commercial center. The manufactures are very extensive, and almost every thing is manufactured here, from a railroad car to a hat. The thrift and enterprise with which every thing is conducted surprise and astonish the stranger. The city has many fine public buildings and beautiful residences. The celebrated stone quarry at Lemont, twenty-five miles south of Chicago, upon the Illinois and Michigan canal, is nearly a milk-white limestone. and forms one of the most beautiful building materials to be found in the western States. I much admire edifices with fronts of this stone. It must attract the attention and command the admiration of all who visit this city.

Of late years the tide of emigration and travel has gone so much around the peninsula, into Wisconsin, Iowa, and northern Illinois, that this beautiful region has been too much overlooked and disregarded by persons traveling either for pleasure or in search of a home in the West. From the fine city of Detroit the entire distance to this magnificent, noble emporium of enterprise and trade, whose growth seems more like magic than reality, is thickly studded with noble farms and pleasant villages. Some of them, like Marshall and Kalamazoo, are unsurpassed for beauty of location, and compare favorably with the most favorable of their class in New England and western New York. The crops this season are good, and the wheat, for which grain no section of the country is better adapted than southern Michigan, turned out a noble and prolific yield. One of the most striking and interesting features in the scenery, to one like myself, seeing it for the first time, are the superb groves and forests of oak, with which the country is studded—many of them clear of underbrush, and the grass close and green as that of a carefully tended park. And yet property is not held so high but that all desirous of purchasing either a village or a country residence in the forest, could do better in central and southern Michigan than in more distant States and Territories. It has a happy medium between a very new and a very old country. The sickness and diseases incident to new settlements have disappeared entirely, while the price of property is not so high as in an old district, and the state of society is equally good, moral, and refined.

XII.

Trip to Charleston.—The Voyage by Steamer.—The Charleston Hotel.—Slavery.—The Arsenal.—The Citadel Academy.

CHARLESTON HOTEL, CHARLESTON, S. C., February 2, 1855.

I SHOULD have written the "Day Book" before, but my engagements have been such I have not had one leisure moment. Our voyage was as speedy as agreeable, the trip being made in forty-eight hours. Two days previous to leaving New York the weather was cold and stormy, but just as the steamer left the pier the clouds faded and parted behind the invisible curtains of air, and were seen no more. The glorious orb, undimmed by a single ray, looked down and smiled his promise upon us; and never was promise better kept: not a cloud was seen the whole passage. With the dark blue deep below, the clear heaven above in the serenity of its azure depths, the magnificent steamer swayed to and fro by the grace of the un-

dulating surface of the waves, and seemed more like a bird skimming the air than a vessel at sea. Never before have I traveled over the same distance with such ease and pleasure. The Nashville is one of the finest boats on the line, and is commanded by that faithful officer and accomplished gentleman, Captain Berry. This steamer has ever been noted for her safe and speedy trips. The only murmur of dissatisfaction I heard on board was that the passage had been too short; and the company invited the captain, in the handsomest manner, to make a pleasure trip without unloading, but he is too great a disciplinarian to be persuaded, even by the ladies.

I am happy to find myself in the care of the gentlemanly host of the Charleston Hotel, Mr. Mixer. I am surprised to find so magnificent a house out of the great metropolis. It is most admirably fitted up, and the best conducted hotel in the city. In the furnishing and decorating, no useless article was admitted, no tasteless ornament introduced. Every thing is complete without superfluity; and here we find the full achievement of an elegant, quiet, comfortable home for the stranger or citizen; and lest I degenerate into an absolute puff,

I will say no more, concluding by simply inviting those visiting Charleston to come to the Charleston Hotel and see if I do not speak truth, when I say it is equal, in all respects, to any other hotel in the Union.

The money pressure is felt here almost as much as in New York. Charleston depends alone on her commerce—her exports, her imports, her receipts and sales of produce from the interior, and the supply afforded in return, for an increase of prosperity. The gale of September did much damage to the crops; in some instances whole plantations were covered by salt water. The prices of cotton have been so low that producers have not sold, and, therefore, the country people have been unable to make their payments to city merchants. Much of the business here is conducted on twelve months' credit. The banks have refused to discount, and the "hard times" fall heavier here upon the merchants. But not so at the North; there the laboring classes feel it most. Here the work is done mostly by negroes, who must be clad and fed, if the master suffers.

I have watched the condition of the slaves here with interest, and I assure you they seem a happy, contented race—comfortably clad and well fed. I feel sure if abolitionists would come South and visit towns, villages and plantations, they would return home with their views changed in regard to Southern institutions. Masters here do not require more than one third of the labor from a slave that a northern man does from a hired servant. The slaves are free from care, and do not even provide for their own offspring. A few days since, in a railroad car, I sat opposite a lady and gentleman traveling with their two little children and slave nurse, who were total strangers to me. They knew not whether I was from the North or South. The lady had provided herself with a small basket of provisions for the accommodation of her little ones, and whenever she offered fruit or cake to her children she invariably gave some to her nurse. Few mistresses at the North would take so much care of their hired nurses.

The African race are as inferior to the white race in intellect as they are in personal appearance. They are wholly incapable of development for self-government or self-protection, and for their own benefit they must be controlled by others. I look upon slavery as a blessing instead of a curse to them, and it is undoubtedly the natural conviction of the negro when he is in juxtaposition with white men. To emancipate them would not be to endow them with the moral or intellectual power to govern themselves or others, but to sink them into the same debasement and misery which mark their truly unhappy condition at the North. The rights of the master and slave are reciprocal under the laws of the South; the right of the master is to the services of the slave for life, and the right of the slave, as secured by law, to humane and proper treatment, to comfortable lodgings, food and clothing, and to proper care in infancy, sickness and old age.

Fanaticism is the most dangerous of all influences to which man is subject. I would beg of abolitionists to stop and pause before inciting slaves to insurrection or asking Congress to legislate upon southern institutions. The southern people are determined to protect their property, and feel bound, as honorable and high-minded men, to have their rights respected, let it cost what it may. They don't ask northerners to adopt or believe in their institutions, but they demand to be let alone. May our Union, like our freedom, be imperishable.

Charleston is a beautiful city. Many of the public and private buildings possess much architectural beauty. The residences here are not molded together by brick and mortar, as they are in our northern cities. There is a retirement, a repose pervading them, which makes them look more like the splendid palaces of opulence and rank, surrounded by the garden of fashion, than the habitations of a commercial city.

I visited the Arsenal and Citadel Academy, and was invited by Major Capers, superintendent and professor, to walk through the establishment. It is modeled after the plan of West Point, and equals that institution in all respects, except in languages. Here are taught but two foreign languages, French and Spanish. The chambers of the two debating societies are richly fitted, containing beautiful banners bearing appropriate inscriptions, a handsome lecture room, etc., etc. On entering the armory (where secession is locked in, but possessing a ready key), the major pointed out two brass field pieces bearing Turkish arms, taken from the Turks by Commodore Decatur, and sold by Mrs. Decatur to the Arsenal of Charleston.

Mayor Hutchison invited me to visit the Council

Chamber. It is very richly and appropriately furnished. On its walls hang full-length portraits of Washington, Calhoun, Jackson, and Taylor. They are all works of considerable merit. In the chamber are also a number of marble busts. Among them is one of Robert Fulton, one of America's gifted sons, which commands attention. It was chiseled by Bremond, a young French sculptor of great talent. It was copied from one in plaster by Houdon, whom Fulton employed to cast, when in Paris from 1802 to 1805. It was presented by J. H. May, a native of South Carolina, to the citizens of Charleston.

The statue of Calhoun, by Powers, is placed in the rotunda of the City Hall. It was shipped on the ill-fated vessel that was wrecked off Fire Island, the one on which the Countess Ossoli was lost. It lay under the water twelve months. It was raised and now stands upon a pedestal, as the image of the bright ornament and spirit that will ever live in the hearts of the American people.

Osgood, the artist, who is at the head of his profession, is here from New York. He has just finished two pictures of great merit—one, a portrait of a young lady and belle of Charleston, the other a portrait of an old gentleman some years since deceased. It was painted from a bust in plaster. It is said by those who were acquainted with the gentleman to be the best likeness ever taken of him. Osgood is winning fresh laurels every year in his beautiful art.

XIII.

Visit to Columbia.—Northern Aggressions.—Beautiful Weather.—Southern Railroads.

UNITED STATES HOTEL, COLUMBIA, S. C., February 12, 1855.

SOUTHERNERS at present have but little to say about secession. The whole South are looking quietly on, watching the movements of the North; but, I assure you, there is a deep under-current of feeling flowing steadily but slowly, as yet invisible to northerners, still its course is sure, and it will swell to the surface and deluge this Union, with misery, and perhaps with bloodshed. And by whom? By those who should still be a band of brothers, who fought side by side, and sacrificed their all for their country's good; whose advancement and prosperity have been much greater than the sanguine hopes of the noble statesmen who formed this confederacy and framed its constitution. Will abolitionists still persist to interfere with southern rights, until forbearance ceases to be a virtue?

There are, no doubt, instances of slaves having tyrannical masters, and being subjected to inhuman treatment; for over the wide, wide werld, there are tyrants in every land and in every clime—husband tyrants, father tyrants—but political tyrants, there should be none. In the hands of our rulers is placed a high and holy trust—their country's welfare—in discharge of which duty they should look to the greatest good to the greatest number. That special endowment, and superior intellect, fitting them for the exalted and responsible position they occupy was not given by divine Providence for their own aggrandizement, but to guide and sway the many, to produce harmony and perfection in the whole body politic.

The South feel that they are constantly misrepresented by northerners, which is too true. Allowing that occasionally a slave is treated with brutality, in all questions exceptions are not rules, it does not argue that it would be right that the whole or any should be emancipated—driven from comfortable homes and protection. The laws of the South protect the slave as well as the master, and are as strictly enforced against him as the slave, if he does not abide by them. Abolitionism had its origin among the descendants of the Puritans, whose forefathers came to this country for conscience' sake—to escape oppression—to worship in freedom, and, as they said, "to be let alone;" and may the descendants of that good and virtuous people remember the spirit which actuated their ancestors, and let others alone.

This is one of the prettiest towns I have ever visited, and I am told by the citizens here that it is healthy at all seasons of the year. It is surrounded by a rolling country, wooded by magnificent white, or what is more properly termed the long-leaf pine. The lumber trade in this State is estimated at half a million a year. This pine not only produces the finest lumber in the United States, but the turpentine extracted from it is another source of great income. The gardens here have ever been the admiration of all travelers, and certainly they surpass any thing I have ever seen in pleasure grounds.

Here all that constitutes the beautiful is put forth in the luxuriance of poetical tracery. Beds and broad walks, fringed with box wood, adorned with the orange, myrtle and pomegranate, and an occasional weeping willow bowing its graceful head, as it were, in admiration of the beauty at its feet. Arbors and summer houses, whose lattices are embowered in vines of rare beauty; ever and anon a flower peeps in, as a welcome messenger of coming spring, while you at the North sit shivering over coal fires, without a flower or green spot to look upon. The most beautiful place here, and the prettiest I have ever seen, is ex-Senator Preston's, although there are a few here that almost equal it in beauty.

The railroads in this State are as good as those North, and as well, if not better, managed. They do not run as fast, but with more safety, and have fewer accidents. The cars are new, kept neat, finely cushioned. On every train is a stewardess to attend to the wants of passengers.

The Columbians say the weather is cold for the season of the year. It seems to me like April. By the papers, I see, on the 7th instant, the thermometer in New York was ten degrees below zero; here it was a mild and beautiful day.

XIV.

Augusta.—The City Hall.—The Church of the Atonement. —Augusta Hotel.

AUGUSTA HOTEL, AUGUSTA, GA., February 22, 1855.

THE South is associated with the romance of my early life. After many years' absence, I have been wont to think of its great rice and cotton fields, its groves of live-oak, magnolia, orange, myrtle, and pomegranate; and its mild climate and softened landscapes have been floating through my imagination like a dream ever since. And now to revisit this section of country, with its varied and most beautiful scenery, is to carry the mind back into the dream-like past—to bring all the romance of youth into vivid reality; and much as the faithlessness of the world has chilled the youthful impulses of my heart, I can not repress the natural sympathy of my breast toward these refined, elegant and noble-hearted people.

This county was originally Saint Paul's parish.

In 1777 it was made the county of Richmond, receiving its name from the Duke of Richmond, a great friend of American liberty. Augusta, its capital, is situated on the south-west bank of the Savannah river, and was named by General Oglethorpe in honor of one of the royal princes. Since the establishment of manufactures, and the completion of its railroads, it having now more than a thousand miles centering in it, few cities have improved more rapidly than Augusta. It is well built, mostly of brick, and favorably situated for trade, being in the center of a thickly populated and wealthy country.

This city has a number of fine public buildings. The City Hall, in Green street, is an ornament to the city. It is built of brick, three stories high, with a cupola surmounted by the figure of Justice. The Medical College is also a fine building. The Masonic Hall is a showy one. In Augusta there are five or six banks, and a number of insurance agencies. The warehouses challenge the admiration of traders. There are ten or twelve of these structures, capable of holding seventy thousand bales of cotton, which were erected at a cost of more than $120,000. The premises belonging to

the Georgia Railroad and Banking Company are worthy the attention of visitors. The freight dépôt is a most conveniently-arranged building. It is two hundred and eighty feet long, and eighty feet wide. The roof projects eleven feet beyond the walls on each side. Cars for receiving the goods stand under the projecting roof upon one side, and the loaded drays drive into all parts of the building through the doors of the opposite side. There are a good number of churches in Augusta. The Church of the Atonement is one of the most unique buildings I have ever seen. It literally seems to be a group of steeples. I am told it was erected at the expense of one family. The Presbyterian Church is a neat edifice, surrounded by a beautiful grove of oaks. The oak is a noble tree; and to me a grove or a tree is a thing to love. Southerners display a refined taste in their buildings. Many of their churches are elegant and tasteful. Their private residences are arranged with an air of comfort. The warm climate makes it necessary to have space, breathing room, which adds much to the beauty and convenience of private dwellings, surrounded as they are by spacious grounds ornamented with rare shrubs, and flowers of great beauty, many of them such as we never see at the North.

I am much pleased with the enterprise and manufacturing spirit of Augusta; for where there is industry and enterprise, there will agriculture and the learned professions thrive. They are as inseparably connected as light and heat, as naturally dependent upon each other as causes and effects. Those who will give citizens good employment are their best friends. Useful employment, and that which is liberally rewarded, is the brightest charity of life. Here they have invaluable staples and immense advantages over the northern States; they have also the same, if not superior, means for cultivating the fine and useful arts. By making more of the necessaries of life among themselves, a vast amount of wealth could be retained here which is now taken from them. If they go on as they have already commenced, they will, in a few years, arrive at such a position as will cause the South to be pointed out among the most flourishing portions of the earth.

There is much said here, as elsewhere, about "hard times." I am told that trade has not been as dull, and money as scarce, for many years, which, no doubt, is true. The epidemic last fall suspended business for two months, and two of the best months for business during the whole year; still, one observes no visible distress; no beggars; no one begging for work, or going to "soup houses." The South have accomplished, in their institution of slavery, what all the French revolutions have been fought for, philosophers have in vain legislated for—labor and security.

The most interesting sight here on Sunday is to watch the black population going to church. Many of them are the most extravagantly dressed people you see in the street. The painly dressed ones wear black silk dresses, white muslin shawls and straw bonnets, or have their heads turbaned in handkerchiefs, tastefully arranged. The men are habited in broadcloth, with bright buttons (they seem to have a *penchant* for bright buttons), fine hats and gloves, cane, and usually a watch and breast-pin. Smiling faces, which display a good set of ivory, and they look, on the whole, very little as if "humanity is crushed out of them," as abolitionists are wont to say. They have here two large African churches, Sunday schools every Sabbath, taught orally, although many of them can read—taught by their young masters and mistresses, when growing up. It is not unusual to see slaves reading newspapers, and familiar with the current news of the day. Slaveholders feel they have a duty to perform toward their slaves, and in most cases discharge the duty like Christian people—training them for civilized life, and teaching them Christianity.

I beg leave to relate an incident which occurred in New York, told to me a few days since by a clergyman of Washington, in this State. He said: "There is living in Washington a free colored man whose family are slaves. The colored man had been desirous to purchase their freedom and emigrate to Liberia. In his anxiety, he asked the clergyman to be kind enough to give him a letter, which he could show to northerners as a reference of his integrity. The clergyman gave him a letter, and he left for the North. When in New York, he accidentally presented it to a celebrated divine and leading abolitionist, whose sister, a lady of great talent, has written a book showing up the worst features of slavery. The divine invited the man to his house, saying his sister could give him a large donation; but she was not in, and he was told to call again and he would get it. He called, but she was out; still the divine held out to him it would be sent on. Six months have passed, and nothing has been received. The colored man said, when North, he presented the letter to many abolitionists, who said they would not give him one cent to purchase their freedom with, but would give thousands to assist them to abscond from their master."

Now this is unpleasant for me to believe of northerners, who profess to be Christians and enlightened people; but I have related it as told to me by a clergyman of high standing. Would Christian abolitionists teach the same crime to the slaves they accuse the masters of—man-stealing? No, no, abolitionists, that won't do; if you are sincere in your philanthropy, you will give thousands to assist them to purchase their freedom with, but not one cent to help them to escape. If they abscond, you will not make them freemen, but criminals, and you a participator, and answerable for that crime. I am happy to inform my readers that the husband has appealed to southerners, and has nearly made up the sum sufficient to purchase his family.

I can not close without paying a well-merited

compliment to the Augusta Hotel, which is under the able management of U. P. Starr, and his assisting clerk, Wm. O. Halloran. Its location is fine and central, convenient to all the dépôts, and is capable of accommodating two hundred and fifty guests. Its tables are profusely furnished with all the luxuries of the season. The rooms are large and well furnished, the house possesses all the modern improvements of eastern hotels. Mr. Starr is a gentlemanly and obliging host. His excellent and superior lady superintends many of the departments of this well-regulated establishment, and to her must be accredited the decided superiority of this house over its rivals. It was the only house in Augusta that was kept open during the epidemic last season. I take much pleasure in commending this house to those who like quiet and substantial comfort, and every thing that the necessities or wants of the traveling public can possibly demand or think of.

Here nature is opening her beauties. The dark gray clouds have rolled away, and the sky assumes a warmer ray. The summer wind whispers in gentle tones, the season's brightness and its warmth are bringing up and producing green foliage, flowers, and fruits. Ten years, at least, melts from the mind by the warm magic of the South, and helps us to forget the frozen climate of the North. Cold winter still settles gloomily around you in New York, and you may yet have to chronicle dozens of sleigh rides and ten degrees below zero. A week ago I saw peach orchards in blossom, and heard the harsh note of the croaking frog.

XV.

En Route for Savannah.—A Southern Sunset.—Loss of Baggage.—The Pulaski Monument.—A "Slave" Funeral.

PULASKI HOUSE, SAVANNAH, March 9, 1855.

I TOOK my seat at Augusta in one of the fine cars of the Waynesborough and Georgia Railroad, on one of the most beautiful days that ever graced a southern clime, and caught with delight a view of a real Claude sunset, from its first glow to the last glimpse of its death shroud. It was a southern sunset, with all its dreamy characteristics, its harmony, its grandeur, its loveliness, and the last gleam of its setting smile playing upon the tall pines sighing to the passing breeze. All things seemed steeped in poetry. The purple and gold, and heaven's own dyes, lay soft and languid upon all around, and breathed into my own heart that sweet contentment and repose which is the only true enjoyment of life.

I arrived in Savannah at half past one in the morning, in the happiest mood, and inquiring for my baggage, I was politely informed by the conductor that it was missing. I expressed some regret and surprise, to which the omnibus driver replied, striding into his seat and giving a crack of the whip, "telegraph—that would bring it." I coolly replied, "I wish it would; I would telegraph to-night, for I am very much in want of it," and drove to the hotel. I alighted and entered, and was shown to my room. As I bolted my door, the question arose in my mind, what am I to do? I have no night toilet. The clock struck two. I unrobed with the serious intention of arising at five, and leave in the first train of cars, in search of my lost trunk. Three hours for sleep!—but what am I to do? what am I to sleep in? A thought suggested itself. I tied a skirt around my neck and turbaned my head in my handkerchief. Catching one glimpse of myself in the mirror, I laughed outright. A pretty good Chinese with my dark brunette face, if the frock was only a blue one; but not being a *bas bleu*, it is a color I never affect. I retired, closing my eyes with the solemn promise, I will sleep. But oh, how those mysterious wheels of the brain moved!—they seemed to be propelled by a six boiler locomotive. Where was that huge black trunk of mine?—that monster to all porters, that has had so many kicks, and cuffs, and tumble downs, on account of its weight, until it looks like a sailor's old weather beaten chest. Had that able-bodied class entered into a conspiracy and sent it on a long errand to get rid of "toting" it up stairs? Shall I ever get it again, and find undisturbed all those tokens of affection—that dear lock of hair, resting so sweetly upon a card inclosed in an envelope, address, "Memento;" all those tender epistles, many of them not containing one word of truth? And then then poetry, the breathings of a tender soul, containing

"So smoothly pass thine hours and years,
So calmly beat thy heart,
While both our souls in concert tuned,
Nor hope nor dream apart."

The miniature, shall I ever see that again? And, above all, shall I ever see that piece of poetry—the only copy in existence—those lines of love upon

MY FADED FLOWER.

I had a fairy little child
With golden hair and eye of blue,
That ever on my bosom smiled—
A beauteous blossom fresh with dew.

The light within her loving eyes
Went to my heart with many a thrill,
Rekindling there the faded dyes
Of youth's fond dreams, all glowing still.

No boyhood's dream of joyousness—
Chivalric love, undying faith—
Had half the strength and power to bless
As my sweet baby's balmy breath.

Her little arms twined around my neck,
Like clinging vines around the oak—
Her dimpling, laughter-rounded cheek
Slept upon mine—on mine it woke.

Her brook-like voice half shaped in words
Of playful fondness, oh, how strong!
My heart made musical, as the birds
Steep the still forest air in song.

She was my soul's bright flower—the star
That from my heart's mysterious deep
Rose like a planet o'er the far
Dark sea, its kindly watch to keep.

The star has set, the sky is dark—
A sense of life hath gone from me;
The dreary world seems sad and stark—
Daughter! I wait to come to thee.

Oh, how my heart-hive swarmed with fancies on the possibility of my never seeing those dear things again! Their value was trifling. Even that ugly miniature grew beautiful in my mind's fancy. At last fancy wore itself out, like fanaticism when let alone; and I was just entering dreamland, when a poor, famished bell, without lungs, which seemed to be hung just outside my window, went tingle dong, tingle dong, tingle dong, and continued for full three quarters of an hour. The only thing it seemed to alarm in the whole city was my poor nerves. I was right glad when it ceased—it was sudden—no passing away sound, as if lost in the stillness of the night, in that unringing thing.

I again withdrew into sweet oblivion, and the scream of "five o'clock!" was the first cause of recurring sense. I started—was soon ready and equipped for my journey. After searching every nook and corner, for several hundred miles around, friends and unknown friends telegraphing hither and thither, I returned to Augusta, and after besieging every baggage room in the city, I went to the telegraph office and telegraphed to the most distant part in the State. It was then ten o'clock in the morning. I inquired, "Shall I receive an answer in an hour?" The wire-worker said, "Perhaps by six o'clock in the evening." I left, thinking telegraphs were slow coaches in this part of the country. However, the answer came in good time, and I returned that night to Savannah, where I received my trunk next day, unlocked it, peeped in, and, much to my delight, all was there—locks of hair, miniature and poetry, in sweet confusion. I breathed more freely. To whom was I indebted for this good luck? Was it the presiding of my good genius or Harnden's express? I came to the conclusion that my thanks were due to Harnden's express. And now my fair and bachelor readers, if you lose your trunk, or have any packages to send or to be brought, I recommend you to Harnden's express. Their business is conducted with care and promptness, and you will have your orders fulfilled in good time, for, I assure you, that is no slow coach. I would say again to my fair readers, if you are put under the care of a handsome and gentlemanly conductor, you will receive every polite attention, but look after your baggage!

Savannah lies on the south side of Savannah

river, built on a plateau of an altitude of about forty feet above the river. It is surrounded by a flat country, interspersed with many swamps, but has a large portion of fertile land. On the river, the tide swamp lands are extensive, and considered the most valuable lands in the State. Many of the rice plantations have a picturesque appearance. There is something in the soil of these rich rice plantations which renders them unhealthy, perfectly destructive to the white population; but I am told that the blacks enjoy on them uninterrupted health.

The colonial and revolutionary associations connected with the history of this section of Georgia are of deep interest. Here General Oglethorpe first landed and commenced the colony of Georgia; here was the first revolutionary battle fought. This city has a number of handsome and imposing public buildings. The Custom House, built of Quincy granite, the Exchange, the hall of the Historical Society, and the State Bank, which is, I think, the handsomest building in the city. Savannah has a large number of churches, and many of them fine and handsome structures. Christ Church is one among the most imposing edifices in Savannah.

5*

The order of architecture is the Grecian Ionic. It has the most classical and chaste façade I have ever seen. The present bishop of the diocese, Stephen Elliot, is its minister.

The Pulaski Monument, in Monterey Square, is the attraction as well as the admiration of all strangers who visit Savannah. It was commenced in 1853, and only finished a few weeks since. It was erected to the memory of Brigadier Count Pulaski, who fell, mortally wounded, at the siege of Savannah, a name dear to the heart of every American, and especially so to the people of Georgia. Count Pulaski was a Polish patriot. This classical and most beautiful marble memorial to his memory, was designed and executed by the gifted and accomplished Lannitz, who has made marble breathe in so many forms of varied beauty. The monument has great purity of style and richness of effect. The design is so perfect, and the execution so artistic, the whole story is conveyed, almost at a glance, to the most unimaginative mind. The coats of arms of Poland and Georgia, surrounded by branches of laurel, ornament the cornice on the front. They stand united together—the eagle, the symbolic bird of both Poland and America, emblem of liberty, independence and courage—rests on both, bidding proud defiance. The cannon on the corners of the die, emblematic of military loss and mourning, give the monument a strong military character. The bands on the shaft are alternately ornamented with the emblems of stars and garlands; the shaft is surmounted by a highly elaborated cap, which adds richness, loftiness and grandeur to the structure. The monument is surmounted by a statue of Liberty, holding the banner of the "stars and stripes." The architectural beauty of the monument, as far as I could judge, is of the highest order, and, beyond question, is the finest monument in America.

Yesterday I paid a visit to Bonaventure, five miles from Savannah, known as the old cemetery, and among the most lovely places in the world. My curiosity to view this deeply engaging spot had been thoroughly excited, as I had often heard it spoken of as an object well worthy the attention of strangers. On entering the cemetery—interesting repository of tombs, and well calculated to awaken our most serious feelings—I was struck with awe at the deep solemnity of this sepulchral scene. Its long, broad avenues of live-oak, from whose bending limbs, stretched in reverential homage over the "honored dead," are suspended, like a pall, the gray moss of this section of country. On one side flows, like a big silent tear, the river; on the other stand tall pines, sighing the harmonious breathings of the light zephyrs, conveying to the imaginative mind the consoling reflection that they are constantly whispering soft requiems over the tenants of the graves which they sentinel. The new cemetery, a mile from the city, is prettily laid out, and has much natural beauty of location and scenery.

In Savannah there is much literary taste, many intelligent and cultivated minds. Education, however, is not extended to the masses here as at the North. The free or common school system in this State is as yet quite imperfect. Those who are educated usually receive a collegiate education; and one meets here many richly endowed and highly cultivated minds. The prosperity that awaits a people depends on the supremacy of mind, on the cultivation of the intellect, on the diffusion of knowledge and the arts; not merely to the chosen few, but to that immense multitude who are at once invested with the privileges of freedom, and the rights of power.

I should have liked to have had a northern abolitionist witness, a few days since, a funeral procession of a colored man, an ordained deacon of the Third Colored Baptist Church of this city. In the procession were four uniformed fire companies. The Porters' Association, of which he was a member, turned out, and wore black scarfs, with white rosettes. I also noticed two or three female benevolent associations, distinguished by suitable dresses. A spectator counted fifty-two carriages, well filled, besides a number on horseback, following the hearse. It is estimated that between two thousand and two thousand five hundred colored persons were in the procession. The procession was perfectly quiet and orderly, and conducted with the utmost decorum. It would be difficult for any working class at the North to get so expensive a funeral. I am told by good authority that the Colored Female Missionary Society in Savannah make much larger donations than the white ladies.

There is no country, and no place upon the face of the globe, where the negro race have such security for a wholesome living, as the slaves in the

United States. The condition of an African slave in America is as far superior to that of a chief on the coasts of Africa, as day is superior to night.

XVI.

Columbus.—The Legend of Lover's Leap, &c.

PERRY HOUSE, COLUMBUS, GA., March 21, 1855.

I FIND so much more to be pleased than displeased with in this beautiful town, I scarcely know what to say. Columbus is an incorporated city of seven or eight thousand inhabitants, situated upon the east bank of the Chattahoochee river. In front of the town ragged and large rocks rise over the whole bed of the river, and convert it into a succession of rapids. Nature displays many sublime and romantic scenes around Columbus; and upon the banks of the river bearing the soft and pretty Indian name, Chattahoochee, many of the landscapes are striking. "Lover's Leap" is a high and ragged cliff, which terminates an ascending knoll of dark rocks projecting over the river, whose weather-beaten front stands out in bold relief, presenting an altitude which, for its precipitous rise, is seldom surpassed, and is well worthy of the attention of travelers. From its summit the city is but partially visible, but it commands a grand display of river scenery. Its beauty, wildness, grandeur, and sublimity would establish the scenic reputation of any locality; and as untrained as my eye is to the beauties of nature, I could sit by the hour and look upon this enchanting spot. The bed of the river is a deep ravine. It flows wild and rapid—broken by rocks and precipices over which the water foams in craggy cascades, strongly reminding one of the rapids of Niagara.

The legend of the "Lover's Leap" is a very romantic story of two young lovers whose attachment and devotion outrivaled that of Romeo and Juliet. They belonged to two powerful but rival tribes of Indians—the Cassetas and Cowetas—who inhabited this section of country in the beginning of the present century. History says the dark-eyed Mohina was the pride of her father's heart, and all his love for the beautiful in life was bestowed on her. The proud chief entertained a bitter hatred towards Young Eagle, the lover to whom was betrothed, when yet a child, his daughter Mohina. Years and feuds had suppressed kindly feelings in the hearts of all save those two young creatures, and the pledged word was broken when the smoke of the calumet was extinguished. The hostilities of the tribes growing more fierce, the young lovers were forbidden to meet. With downcast look and softly-vailed anxiety Mohina consented to abscond with her lover. With undaunted courage they fled "with love's light wings," for pure love dwelt in their hearts, and base fear crouched low before it. They were pursued. Love and terror added strength and speed to their flight, but the strength of the maiden failed in a perilous moment, and had not Young Eagle snatched her to his fast-beating heart, the enemy had made sure their fate. He rushed onward until he gained this fearful height, turned for a moment, cast a triumphant look on his enemies, and the next, with the beautiful Mohina still clinging to him, leaped into the surging stream below. The projecting rock, embossed with dark foliage, hangs as it were in grief over the shrines of the departed lovers, and still perpetuates the sad recollection of those who were one in heart and one in death. Long since the Great Spirit called the old chief in sorrow and broken-hearted from the council fire to join the young lovers in the spirit land.

Having half an hour of leisure, the other day,

I visited the daguerrian gallery in Broad street, and was most politely received by the accomplished artist, J. Andrew Riddle. I was much gratified but surprised to find such artistic and life-like pictures. They compare favorably with those of the best daguerrian artists in New York. The universal accessibility of this art to all, renders it valuable to those who are debarred of possessing themselves of more expensive portraits. In the daguerreotype is fulfilled the long promise of art through ages, and the sunbeam becomes the pencil in the hand of that greatest of all artists, Nature.

I saw there many excellent likenesses of distinguished American citizens—Edwin Forrest, the American tragedian; Saroni, the musical composer; General Tom Thumb, in martial array; Mrs. Caroline Lee Hentz; and the lamented Mrs. Welby, whose sweet poetry is familiar to many. One among the most attractive in the gallery is a correct likeness of Colonel Lomax, who was an officer in the Mexican army, at present editor and proprietor of the Columbus "Sentinel and Times." It would be difficult for the artist to do more than justice, and much less flatter the original. The colonel possesses a handsome face, expressive of the highest order of intellect, a *distingué* and engaging manner. He is also a bold and vigorous writer, without a trace of the audacity and extravagance which is so much in vogue with American journalists. In all he shows an appreciative, refined and delicate taste. He is a leading politician in this State, a man of great excellence and worth of character, is highly esteemed by the citizens of Columbus, and one of whom the South may be justly proud.

No country is more highly favored with water facilities than Muscogee county. Chattahoochee river, in ordinary seasons, is navigable for nine months of the year to the Gulf of Mexico; but the past fall and winter the river has been so low as to suspend navigation until a few days since. In all probability, in a few weeks the pulses of trade will begin to beat, now that the big vein of the country, which circulates life and vigor through its system, is in full and healthy action. Cotton will be exported, merchandise imported, and those clever and handsome merchants in Broad street will send out their dainty circulars of invitation, which will be acknowledged in fashionable calls by those very pretty and interesting ladies (Columbus has not a few), and they soon will be robed in muslins and laces transparently beautiful, and when used discreetly, and with taste, so much heighten and bring out a woman's natural charms and gifts of person. I shall ever retain a pleasing remembrance of the interesting ladies of the Perry House and their kind and delicate attentions; and may the pretty Mrs. C—— ever remain as beautiful as the flowers she presented me. Among the pleasant acquaintances I have made in this city is Dr. Thomas W. Grimes, celebrated for his anti-dyspeptic medicine, so highly appreciated by all suffering from that complaint, who have been so fortunate as to procure it for use. Dr. G. is a physician of the old school, and is one of the most extensive and successful practitioners in Georgia.

The soil of this country varies from the richest vegetable mold to the poorest sand. There are several fine public buildings in Columbus, among which are the Court House, Odd Fellows' Hall, and Methodist Church. The Methodist is the largest religious sect in this city. A few ladies of the Methodist church projected and erected "The Columbus Female Asylum." It is educational and benevolent in its scope. The necessary funds, in the beginning of the enterprise, were raised in part by the needle. In 1848, upon invitation, a limited number from the other denominations of the city cheerfully united, and it is now in a most flourishing condition, the good work going on with Christian zeal, and has already gladdened the heart of many an orphan.

Columbus has several factories of large capital in successful operation. The buildings are a credit to the owners. Almost every thing is manufactured here, from the cotton gin to the churn—every kind of cotton and woolen goods—all kinds of writing, printing and wrapping paper.

I am glad to see the South becoming more and more enterprising, and, therefore, more independent every year, by manufacturing more of the necessaries of life among themselves—establishing a reciprocal sympathy and fellow-interest among all classes of society; in short, making one dependent upon another, which is the only true secret of happiness and prosperity.

I would call public attention to this first class hotel, the Perry House. It is new, rooms large, pleasant and comfortably furnished, table excellent.

Strangers wishing to spend a few weeks South, I would recommend Columbus, being a healthy and dry climate, and just the place where one could pass their time pleasantly and agreeably.

XVII.

A Trip to Saint Louis.—Detroit.—The Towns of Michigan.—Chicago.—Illinois.—Prairies.—Saint Louis.

PLANTERS' HOUSE, SAINT LOUIS, June 16, 1855.

AT the present time, a trip from New York to Saint Louis is no difficult thing, but a pleasant enjoyment, attended with less fatigue than a jaunt of a hundred miles a few years since. The Hudson River Railroad connects at Albany with the Great Central route, including the New York Central, Great Western, Michigan Central, and Chicago, Alton and Saint Louis, forming an entire and perfect line of railroad, and far the best and shortest route from New York to Saint Louis. By calling at the office, 173 Broadway, New York, one can procure from the polite and accomplished agent, Darius Clark, Esquire, a ticket which will, in an incredibly short space of time, take you from the bustle and noise of New York to the "Far West," by Niagara, and over the "Suspension Bridge"—

two of the greatest wonders of the new world. Few men are so highly esteemed as Mr. Clark. He possesses considerable literary taste, is a man of great excellence of character, and has made himself famous by ferreting out that gang of desperadoes, the Michigan Central Railroad conspirators. It was he who had all the arrests made, and carried the whole thing successfully through. If he shows as much administrative ability and powers of calculation in his present agency, the success of the road will be unparalleled.

I left Albany, that Dutch aristocratic capital, at eleven o'clock on the morning of the 29th of May, and passed up that fertile and highly-cultivated region, the valley of the Mohawk. The coming summer, the lovely foliage, the rural scenery of field, and orchard, and meadow, and fine crops, that now look well, and promise a bountiful harvest, and all the gay pomp of June, present beauties and repose to the traveler. His thoughts are elevated and inspired by contemplating this picture by the greatest of all artists—Nature.

Twelve hours from Albany to Niagara, some three hundred and fifty miles! Truly, the iron horse makes neighborhoods of distances. I arrived

at the Falls at eleven o'clock, and tarried for the night.

The next morning, after taking a look at the "Falls" and Bridge, I took my seat in the cars for Detroit. The country, through the whole route, is rolling and fertile, new, but fast filling up; and the crops look well. If one can judge by the specimens they see by the wayside, they have a mixed community—Canadians, French, English, run-away negroes, and a few Yankees. Detroit is a fine city, and I found the Biddle House the same elegant and comfortable place it has ever been since its opening.

The route from Detroit to Chicago passes through many beautiful towns. Ann Arbor, Jackson, Marshall, Kalamazoo, Niles and Michigan City, are all towns of importance, and many of them gems—spots of earth upon which the eye can feast. At Marshall travelers get a most excellent dinner. Every thing is conducted with such order, taste and decorum, that one imagines he is dining in a fashionable hotel.

I spent three days at Kalamazoo, and I saw the town and country to the best advantage at this delightful season. Every thing is filled with blos-

6

soms and flowers of spring: they looked like charming retreats, upon which memory loves to linger. The village contains about ten thousand inhabitants, located upon a burr-oak plain; and the early settlers left standing many of the forest trees, whose lofty tops and wide-extending branches now add greatly to the beauty of the place. The residences are neat and tasteful, surrounded with grounds filled with shrubs and flowers. Some of the public buildings possess considerable architectural beauty; and there are some fine ones in process of erection.

Toward evening of a beautiful day, in company with a dear and interesting friend, I visited the cemetery, situated upon an eminence half a mile from the town, sufficiently removed from its noise for retirement and calm reflection. It is carpeted with the delightful livery of nature; and still are the forest trees sighing in the passing breeze, as it were in grief over the shrines of those that lay interred at their feet. There is a variety of memorials—and some of them very beautiful—that are here erected to perpetuate the fond recollections of those who were beloved in life. The view of the town from this spot is very picturesque. It looks like a city with tall spires, nestled in a deep wood. The distant finishing which nature has given to the picture is seldom found in American scenery.

From Kalamazoo I took the cars for Chicago, where I arrived the same evening, and went direct to the Tremont House, and found it thronged, as usual. This house seems to me to be a world's fair to show up live specimens of humanity, and they always have on hand an extraordinary variety. Such a motley set! You meet there the nobleman and his suite; the backwoodsman in his coarse clothes and fur cap (all the same, June or January); the illustrious lady and party, over dressed; the German woman with her toys and wares for sale; and all seem to have the same object in view, a hurry to get in, and anxious to get away. And there stands the identical stalwart porter, in what seems to be the area of the house, between the office and the reception room, calling out, at the top of his deep bass voice, at intervals of every ten minutes during the twenty-four hours, "All for the Michigan Central," "all for the Milwaukie boat," "all for the Rock Island road," until he calls over the name of almost every place in the Union.

In all this hubbub, I got left—did n't go in the first coach, but sent for an extra one and hurried down to the dêpót, and there found several trains abreast. I inquired which was the St. Louis train; it was pointed out; I stepped in and took my seat, congratulating myself on not being left. The train soon started, and the conductor came round to look after his fare; showed him my ticket, and to my surprise the handsome dandy informed me I was on the wrong train. I of course was left at the first station, but railroads in that section are very near neighbors, and fortunately for me the St. Louis train was fifteen minutes behind, and with an extra signal I got on board. It was a long train, eighteen cars and one horse, and proved rather a slow coach.

That morning four hundred United States troops left Chicago, bound for Kansas, all armed with a tin cup and a long pipe. It was a comical sight to see them leave the cars at every station, and run in their stiff regimentals, tin cup in hand, for dear life, as if the enemy was at their heels. If the crops fail in that section this year, I shall not be surprised—the consumption of water that day was enough to produce a drought for the next two years.

It is almost worth a trip from New York here to see the magnificent prairies of Illinois. They seem almost as vast as the ocean; but not like the sea, they do not inspire sublimity. For miles and miles, not a habitation, tree or shrub to be seen—nothing but the green, delightful carpet of Natnre, and the blue sky mottled with soft white clouds. On the line of the railroad the country will soon be settled; it is now fast filling up. In many parts of the State of Illinois lands have been in the hands of speculators and held at a fictitious value, and that, no doubt, is the reason so much valuable land remains unsettled.

St. Louis is a noble and enterprising city, containing 120,000 inhabitants, and well built. The public buildings and business houses are nearly all fine, and many of them magnificent structures. A large number are constructed of "Missouri marble," and readily attract the eye of a stranger as he passes along Fourth street. Alongside of those marble buildings are others recently finished, which are also very ornamental, and mostly built of "Missouri iron," two natural productions which Missouri has in great abundance. St. Louis also has a fine back country, possessing the richest soil, and not only that, but her sister States—such as Iowa and Wisconsin—pouring their mine of wealth into the lap of St. Louis. In various parts of the city are dwellings that *are really palaces.* One peculiarity in all kinds of buildings here, is the absence of any mere tinsel work, designed only for show. There is less of any thing bordering on *ethereal.* Every thing is done for permanency; all business here seems to be founded on a sure basis; but few banks; all trade being dependent on its own resources.

The environs of St. Louis are very beautiful, and the drives pleasant. The "Belle Fontaine Road," on which is located the Belle Fontaine Cemetery, five miles from the city, has great natural beauty of location, new and, as yet, not much cultivated. Hyde Park is a place of great resort—grounds prettily laid out, ornamented with beautiful shade trees, flowers, and every thing which makes it pleasant and interesting to the visitor. In this magnificent park, of a fine evening, promenade owners of magnetic eyes and graceful forms, attended by *distingué* looking gentlemen, and along the walks leap groups of lovely and laughing children, arrayed in all a mother's pride condensed into the quaintest and most picturesque costume that ever fairy milliner imagined.

The Planters' House is on the corner of Fourth, Chestnut and Pine streets, and one of the most delightful locations in the city, kept by pleasant and well-bred men. Of all the hotels I have ever visited, this is one of the finest and best-managed establishments, and is *the* hotel of St. Louis. The rooms are all spacious, airy, and well appointed. Two fine dining saloons—tables profusely furnished with all the luxuries of the St. Louis market (which are not a few,) and served in perfect order and elegance. It is not surprising that the Planters' Hotel has become so widely known and always well filled, and this passing notice is justly due to the house and to those interested in its management.

At present almost the only topic of conversation here is the failure of the house of Page & Bacon, and the Ohio and Mississippi railroad. The city of St. Louis has stock to the amount of $300,000. The county of St. Louis $200,000. Besides this sum subscribed by the city and county to this road in their corporate capacity, by individuals in said city and county, $271,000, making in all $771,000. This whole sum is likely to be lost, and attributable mainly, as it is said, to the mismanagement of the road. As Messrs. Page & Bacon had the control and management of the finances of the company, much indignation has been felt and uttered against

said firm, is pronounced gross and infamous libels, and that they are high-minded and honorable men —so you see they have here warm friends and bitter enemies, and it is impossible for a stranger to judge who is right or wrong.

XVIII.

Western Railroads. — The Hoosiers. — Filthy Cars. — Advice to Conductors. — Indiana. — Louisville. — Its Growth. — Politics. — Louisville Hotel.

Louisville Hotel, Louisville, Ky., October 24, 1855.

I LEFT the great central route, including New York Central, Great Western, and Michigan Central, forming a perfect line of railroad, and the best managed in the country, at Michigan City, and took the Salem and Albany road to Louisville. This road is new, but seems well managed. The conductor on the train, Mr. Harrison, proved himself to be a most gentlemanly and vigilant man. The road crosses the entire State of Indiana. This almost telegraphic speed of railroad traveling changes in a few hours the romance of childhood and the recitations of the school room into a vivid reality. The great lakes, rivers and prairies of the West have been fixed in my imagination since my earliest remembrance, and I have been wont to think of them as untraveled regions to be seen only by the bold pioneer or the Indian, who ventured in his frail bark upon their deep clear waters. Now a trip West is no difficult or strange thing. Comparatively speaking, in a few hours, we are taken from the gay metropolis, with all its enchantments, its show and extravagances, its beautiful ladies and handsome gentlemen, with fascinating and pleasing manners, cultivated as they generally are at the expense of frank-hearted sincerity.

Our judgments are formed less from reason than from sensation; and as sensation comes to us from the outward world, so we find ourselves more or less under its influence, and little by little we imbibe a portion of our habits and feelings from it. It is not then without cause that when we wish to judge of a stranger beforehand, we look for indications of his character in the circumstances which surround him. The things among which we live are necessarily made to take our image, and we unconsciously leave on them a thousand impressions of our minds. As we can judge by the imprint of the shoe in the sand the size of the foot that wears it, so the abode of every man discovers to a close observer the extent of his intelligence and the feelings of his heart.

Some of the people in the interior of Indiana are uncouth, and possess unbounded curiosity. As soon as they enter the car they give you a most searching stare, and immediately ejaculate, "You traveling?" You answer in the affirmative. They wish to know where; you tell them, and they say, "On a visit?" If you answer by stating you are going to a more distant point, their stare of intense curiosity, if more intelligible, would annihilate you, and strongly reminds one how the children used to gaze at the elephant and the monkey away up in Vermont, I won't say how many years ago, when an elephant and monkey in those primitive days made a whole menagerie. When these well-meaning people get forty miles from home, they talk of the accomplishment as a greater feat than we think that of the allies in taking Sevastopol, if they had not been so long about it. The men all chew tobacco—not only their lips and teeth are dyed with the disgusting weed, but their clothes also, and the floor of the car is deluged with the saliva, upon which float apple-parings and other deposits, until the odor is insufferable, and makes one feel like beating a retreat, and long for "sweet purification." They not only seem to think the car a coach of conveyance, but a box for contributions of every disgusting filth. If I were conductor, I'd put up cards of regulations. "Tobacco deposits—heinous offense;" "apple-parings and paw-paws—heavy fine;" and so on to the minor nuisances down to the crumbs of bread and cheese. The human animal has no more right to chew tobacco and strew nuisance upon the floor of a public conveyance, at the expense of other people's comfort, than he has in a public parlor.

Indiana is a fine State, possessing superior land. The north-western part is flat, with large prairies; the south-eastern part rolling, with varied and beautiful scenery, well wooded and watered. On the line of the railroad, seven miles north of Lafayette, is the old battle ground where General Harrison conquered the Indians. It is walled in, or rather boarded in to resemble a wall. There are still standing many of the forest trees pierced with balls, showing the mis-hits at the Indians. A few poor soldiers rest their heads peacefully pillowed, who lost their lives in this struggle, and I understand there is soon to be erected a monument to the memory of an officer who fell in this battle.

Louisville is not increasing so rapidly as in former years, but its growth is sure and steady. Within a year or two there has been a decided improvement in the architecture of the city. Main street has become lined with splendid business houses; a fine new hotel has just been erected; a Baptist church, the finest in the city, costing $90,000, is about being completed; a very extensive Masonic Temple, occupying an entire square, is being finished; and the largest and costliest custom house in the West is in process of erection.

The people of Louisville are chiefly devoted to commercial pursuits, and a great deal of capital is invested in steamers. Manufacturing establishments, however, are growing. Two railroads, one to Lexington, and the other to Nashville, center here. Another to Memphis is spoken of, while those on the opposite shore of the river afford every facility for quick transit to the North and East.

There are about sixty churches, the Methodist being most numerous; two flourishing medical colleges; a law school; and an unrivaled system of common school education.

The Louisville Hotel is by far the most elegant and complete hotel I have found in the whole western country. It possesses all modern improvements, and every arrangement is calculated to contribute to the comfort and convenience of guests. The proprietor, Mr. Kean, is a very agreeable, entertaining and energetic gentleman, and has the ability, and succeeds in making himself a most excellent host. Strangers visiting Louisville should by all means remember this house, where they will not only be surrounded with the necessities but the luxuries of life.

XIX.

A Visit to Frankfort.—The State Capitol.—The Cemetery.—The Military Monument.—Daniel Boone.—Governor Morehead.

CAPITOL HOTEL, FRANKFORT, KY., November 12, 1855.

THE trip from Louisville to Frankfort is not made with the telegraphic speed we travel on some of the eastern roads, but with more care and caution, hence fewer accidents to chronicle in which "nobody is to blame." The cars are fine, the roads smooth, and managed with ability and energy. The face of the country on the line of the road is gently undulating, excepting "the beech flats," and some portions intersected by small streams, which are uneven and hilly.

Frankfort, the capital of the State, is beautifully situated on the Kentucky river, sixty miles above its mouth, and nestled in the midst of the wild and romantic scenery which renders this stream so noted. From the tops of the overhanging cliffs, which environ the plain beneath like the bastion curtains of a mighty castle, the city of Frankfort and the town of South Frankfort, with their public edifices and private residences, their spires and gardens, and the graceful stream which, like a silver thread, sweeps through the green valley, are all spread out to the eye in a single view of varied and picturesque beauty. The State House, with the public offices on either side of it, is situated on a slight eminence, about half way between the river, which it fronts, and the northern termination of the valley. It is a large and handsome structure, built of Kentucky marble, with a portico in front, supported by six columns of the Ionic order. The Senate and Representative halls are large rooms, beautifully finished and furnished. The walls are ornamented with portraits, one of General Washington, life size; one of General Lafayette, which is really a work of great merit; and also those of Colonel Daniel Boone and General William Henry Harrison. In the governor's office I saw a smaller portrait of Daniel Boone, said to be the only correct likeness extant. It was painted in 1819, in the last years of his life, when in feeble health, by a celebrated American artist, who visited him in

Missouri for that purpose. I am told when the artist reached there he found the old hardy pioneer reclining on his bed, and a slice of venison twisted round the rammer of his rifle, within reach of his hand, was roasting before the fire. The expression of his countenance in this picture is one of firm purpose, but of kind heart. The public offices are plain, but neat and substantial buildings. The public grounds embrace an area of some four or five acres, and are studded with a variety of handsome shrubs and forest trees. In front of the capitol is a beautiful fountain. The governor's house is a large, plain brick building.

I am indebted to his Excellency Governor Morehead for a visit to the cemetery. It is situated in the north-eastern precincts of the city, sufficiently removed from its noise and bustle for retirement and calm reflection, upon a high eminence, on the bank of the river, overlooking the city and valley, and the beautiful surrounding country. Its long, broad avenues of handsome forest trees, their waving tops sighing in the passing breeze, as it were, in grief over the shrines of those that are interred at their feet. The beauty of memorials that are here erected to perpetuate the fond recollections of those "who were beloved in life, and sainted in the grave," far exceeded my expectations. This city of silent inmates is arranged in the most appropriate and convenient manner, so as to permit a procession, even in carriages, to approach within a few feet of every grave.

While wandering among these glass-clad avenues I observed a variety of beautiful shrubbery. The "solemn yew," that sorrow-stricken tree which pines in the night breeze over the solitary dead; the cypress, emblem of mourning; but an absence of the weeping willow, to shed its melancholy yet pleasing influence around. There is an indescribable beauty connected with this sensitive tree, which renders it peculiarly suitable as an appendage to the sanctuary of the dead—its bending form rustling with the slightest agitation; and when the living mourners assemble beneath its waving canopy, may they not conceive by a rather strong figure of prosopopœia, that the harmonious breathings of the light zephyrs, as they struggle through its luxuriant foliage, cause it to sympathize with the bereaved feelings which lacerate their own breasts?

In the Frankfort cemetery, by an act of the

Legislature, was erected, on the State mound, the Military Monument. It was designed and executed by Mr. Robert E. Launitz, of New York. I shall attempt, without a hope, however, of doing justice, or being successful, to give a general outline of the features of this beautiful work of art. The main structure stands upon a base of beautiful Connecticut granite, elegantly chiseled, and twenty feet square at the base. The material of the monument itself is the purest marble, free from all blemishes, and perfectly uniform in color, imported expressly for the purpose from a celebrated quarry at Carrara, Italy.

On the front, and first tablet above the base, is inscribed—"Military Monument, erected by Kentucky, A. D. 1851." Reverse side—"Kentucky has erected this column in gratitude, equally to her officers and soldiers." On the other side, the principal battles and campaigns, in which her sons devoted their lives to their country, are inscribed on the bands, and beneath the same are the names of her officers who fell. "The names of her soldiers who died for their country are too numerous to be inscribed on any column." North side—"By order of the Legislature, the name of Colonel

J. J. Hardin, of the 1st Regiment Illinois Infantry, a son of Kentucky, who fell at Buena Vista, is inscribed hereon."

These tablets are set in panel work on which are carved beautiful figures, to be hereafter noticed. Above and surrounding these is an elegantly carved cornice, extending out several inches, the shading of which is deep and of exquisite sculpture. On each corner of this cornice block stands the colossal figure of an eagle, symbolic bird of America—emblem of liberty, independence and courage, bidding proud defiance. These noble representations of one of the nation's emblems, standing, as they do, in bold relief as guards to each corner of the die, will always attract marked attention. The coat of arms of Kentucky, surrounded by a representation of the rays of the sun, stands between these eagles on the front and reverse sides, with the inscription over the hunters, who are clasping each other's hands and shoulders, "United we stand, divided we fall." Then comes the pedestal block of the column.

As stated in the inscription above, the names of the battles in which Kentuckians were engaged are inscribed on the bands between each block, and on the blocks below, the names of officers who fell in those battles. The names are too many for me to write out. There are no inscriptions on the north side above the tablet, the Legislature having directed that places should be left to be filled up hereafter.

The artist has beautifully illustrated the design in the ornaments and statues. As a whole, it seems to me the most beautiful idea ever conceived by man, and does much credit to the taste of Kentuckians. It is erected in the center of the mound, and beneath its shadow rests peacefully the illustrious dead who have fallen in the numerous battles in which the noble sons of Kentucky have been engaged. Thus, the figures on the front panel on each side of the tablet represent Civic and Military Fame, the one holding the branch of oak, and the other laurel. They blow their trumpets to make known the valiant deeds of the fallen, and to call upon rising generations to imitate the noble deeds and virtues of their fathers. On the reverse side are History and War—war concluded, victory won—the sheath, sword and wreath of laurel; the soldier's meed in one hand, and handing her trophy to History, as if to say, "It is your task now to put my deeds on your record."

The cap of the column is composed of the palm-leaf, always an emblem of reward for merit. Military arms, by the side of which are cannon, and cannon balls, giving the monument a strong military character, are placed over the cap, and over these the banners which floated over them while gaining death and victory. The monument is surmounted by a statue of Victory, her drapery flowing in graceful folds, standing elevated on a pedestal several feet above all else, and seems in the act of ratifying, with her crowns in hand, the award paid to the illustrious dead, whose lives were freely given for the honor and defense of their country. It is inferior in magnificence of proportion to several other public monuments in America; but for beauty of proportion, elegance of design and material, and taste and genius displayed in adornments and execution, there is nothing to surpass it, I believe nothing to equal it, in this country. It is a created poem, beautiful as a fancy dream of a young painter. It not only illustrates the virtues and noble deeds of the fallen patriots of the State in a durable and handsome manner, but it is an evidence that her people can appreciate the beautiful in art, at the same time they are representing the patriotic impulses of their constituency; and it will immortalize the inspiration of the gifted and accomplished Launitz, who has already made marble breathe in so many forms of varied beauty.

My greatful thanks are due to that polished gentleman, Judge Mason Brown, Secretary of State, for a fine picture of this exquisite monument.

A short distance from the mound on which stands the Military Monument, is another by the same artist, and equally as fine a piece of sculpture, to commemorate the memory of Colonel Richard M. Johnson.

The remains of Colonel Daniel Boone, and those of his wife, were removed from the State of Missouri and rest in this interesting spot, peacefully pillowed, without a tombstone, under the shadow of two fine sycamore trees; and the only things that mark the spot are a clump of cane, and a semicircle of rough rocks and stumps promiscuously thrown together. This, no doubt, is an appropriate memorial to his memory, as he was one who ever flew before civilization. Still, I think there should be some memorial erected by which a stranger would recognize his resting-place.

The citizens of Frankfort are a polite, courteous

people, with great suavity of manner, blended with grace and polished dignity. Many distinguished families reside here. Among them the talented ex-Governor Crittenden, whose pretty wife was known, a few years since, in fashionable circles, as the handsome and fascinating Mrs. General Ashley. She is still mistress of her many charms. There are an unusual number of beautiful ladies here, and all with whom I have met have gentle and pleasing manners.

Governor Morehead, who fills the executive chair of Kentucky, is a truly accomplished man. He has a noble and commanding figure, and a handsome and pleasing countenance. He is a whig, but popular with all parties; and all are ready to acknowledge that the man honors the place full as much as the place honors the man, and one of whom Kentucky may justly be proud.

Kentucky has the best climate, and embraces some of the finest lands and most beautiful scenery, of any State in the Union. She is midway between the North and the South, and may she prove a knot tied by her noble sons to hold together and cement in good feeling the union of the States—the rock of our salvation. American spirit, which once defied and resisted British oppression, should become pride. Let it never be recorded of Americans, that after having overcome the greatest difficulties, and gained the admiration of the whole world by their valor and policy, they lost their acquired reputation, their national consequence and happiness, by their own indiscretion.

The Constitution is not feeble: it is yet fresh and strong. Nothing has come to cause its dissolution but abolition fanaticism. Like the granite rock on the ocean strand, which drives back the ceaseless waves that assail its base, will every Union-loving heart resist the assaults made upon it, come how or whence they may.

The Capitol Hotel is a new, large, pleasant and well-appointed house. Its table is profusely furnished, and served with much taste and elegance. Strangers wishing to spend a few weeks in Kentucky, will find the Capitol Hotel just the place where one can pass their time pleasantly and agreeably.

XX.

Steamboat Traveling.—Southern Scenery.—Southern Hospitality.—Growth of New Orleans.

St. Charles Hotel, New Orleans, December 20, 1855.

My journey from Louisville to New Orleans has been much more agreeable than my previous experience of some years since had led me to expect. We talk of the march of intellect—the progress of intellect—the progress of the age, but the extravagance of living, and the conveniences for traveling, supersede all other advancements. I took passage on the "Belle Sheridan," one of the finest boats on the river, commanded by the gallant and obliging Captain Key. The accommodations on this boat are equal to the best regulated hotels, and the journey of fifteen hundred miles was achieved in this floating palace with perfect ease and comfort. Her state rooms are larger and better furnished than some of the single rooms in the fashionable hotels of New York. She had seventy-five or a hundred passengers, and a more happy or merry party I have seldom met. The only murmur of dissatisfaction I heard was the trip had been too short, whereupon the company invited Captain Key, in the handsomest manner, to make a pleasure excursion without unloading, but he is too great a disciplinarian, and too successful in commanding "a Belle" to be persuaded even by the ladies.

The scenery is interesting and picturesque for a hundred and fifty miles above New Orleans. There is something indescribably agreeable in the smooth and boundless expanse of unrivaled fertility, whose dim outline mingles with the blue of the far-off Gulf—the whole vast plain covered by immense fields of sugar cane, the richest staple of America, with occasional rice patches waving in the breeze. Then, too, we see orange groves laden with ripe and golden fruit—trees of the live oak and magnolia, surrounding neat white mansions, the abodes of wealth, comfort, and hospitality—summer houses of oriental architecture, wreathed with the rarest vines and flowers, and innumerable cattle and horses grazing in the fields, or reposing here and there under the shade of the wooded points. Although not prolific, like the North and West, in hill and dale, cliff and cascade, alternately varying and beautifying the landscape, yet the South enchains and fascinates as truly as if the "enchanter's wand" had been at work and transformed what may have been the ocean, or connecting together floating prairies, had created this vast and beautiful Elysium.

The last day of the journey was the Sabbath—a day so soft and fine that nature seemed carpeted with emerald and bordered with flowers of a thousand hues. The rose clustering with the jessamine, appeared to repose in the beauty of holiness, fanned by the breath of heaven filled with sweet incense. I lingered on deck many hours, wooed by the bland atmosphere of this latitude and the beauty around, as the boat glided smoothly along upon the waves of the great highway to the ocean. In my reverie my mind reverted back to the time when De Soto, the Spanish adventurer, discovered these waters. Men have changed, forests have fallen, cities have risen, and the red man has followed the buffalo to the far-off mountains, where he may look upon the setting sun and muse upon his fate; but still the Mississippi is the same. The old trees I see floating upon the stream, where grew they? How many miles has that old log traveled from the spot where its sprig first peeped out upon the wooing sunbeam?

How many years since the midnight blast tore it from the mountain side? and at how many islands and banks has it rested till lifted again by the swelling flood to speed once more upon its journey? Like its course upon the waves, generations are speeding along the tide of time, hurrying onward to the eternal ocean. Nothing charmed me more than watching the distant landscape fading away in the soft twilight of a southern sky, more like some fancied creation than a reality. There are those who have no music in their souls, but I doubt if there lives one so sublimely stupid, so unenviously apathetic, so malignly indifferent, as not to feel somewhat more than mere existence as he floats upon this grand river, and contemplates in silence the luxuriant beauty of its banks in this dreamy atmosphere.

Often when the boat stopped, the passengers would stroll upon the bank to some neighboring mansion, where plenty and hospitality seemed ever to reign. The kind hostess would invite them to her garden —a December picture in nature!—filled with fruits and flowers, and I am sure more beautiful than those of lost Paradise, or mother Eve never would have had that last talk with the beguiling serpent. I saw at one gathering, forty bouquets without marring the picture—each one of which would have cost in New York, in these holiday times, twenty dollars. How our modern belles would have coveted them to decorate their magnificent parlors for the coming New Year! I here gladly make my cordial thanks to the beautiful and accomplished Miss K——, of Kentucky, for the exquisite bouquet she presented me, and the speech delivered with such *naïveté* and grace from her rosy lips. May her pure and spotless mind ever shed upon the world a perfume as rare and delicate as the flowers she culled for me.

New Orleans has greatly improved in architectural taste since my last visit, in '42. The city is now under one municipal government, and there seems to be more union of feeling between the French and American population. It is strictly a busy, bustling commercial city—to the South what New York is to the North. The general health is good. The weather warm—musquito bars requisite, but not fires. Strangers are flocking here in crowds to pass the winter on business or pleasure, and both have a promising beginning. The French theater is open with attractive programmes. A new prima donna, Madame Colson, is playing here to large houses. Hackett, a week since, finished a most successful engagement at the St. Charles. The Gaiety and the Pelican are doing well. Mademoiselle Rachel is expected here soon. People are rubbing up their French and studying beforehand the plays she acts in order to understand her. I predict here will be her greatest success in this country. The French population are in ecstacy about her, and those who neither understand her language nor her talent, will enjoy her acting from the influence of the sensation produced by those around them.

XXI.

The Saint Charles.—New Orleans in Winter.—A Fashionable Lady's Daily Routine.—Mrs. General Gaines.—The New Custom House.—Free Schools.

SAINT CHARLES HOTEL, NEW ORLEANS, January 1, 1856.

NEW ORLEANS can boast of one of the finest hotels in America. In magnificence and beauty of proportion, elegance of design and material, and taste displayed in architectural adornment and execution, there is nothing in the hotel line in this country exceeds the Saint Charles; and it affords an evidence that the citizens of New Orleans can appreciate the beautiful as well as the comforts and elegances of living. The interior of the building surpasses the exterior, if possible. In furnishing and decoration the parlors no useless article was admitted, no foolish ornament was introduced. Every thing is complete, without superfluity. The bedrooms are large, and tastefully furnished with every convenience. There are three dinners served each day, so that one can suit his own time and convenience in taking meals and refreshment. The "ordinaries" are elaborately finished, and elegantly furnished with tables set with rich plate and crystal, that would do honor to any nobleman's palace. Those who visit New Orleans should go to this magnificent establishment, and place themselves under the care of those agreeable and gentlemanly men, the Messrs. Hall and Hilldreth, the proprietors of this excellent house. In winter, the Saint Charles compares favorably with the United States at Saratoga, in summer, in gayety and fashion; and wherever we are, or under whatever sky we move, woman is, after all, an interesting problem, well worth the studying, especially if you have nothing else to do. And strange, piquant and peculiar as may be her habits, her appearance and her caprices elsewhere, it is only at these gay, fashionable gatherings, where talent, beauty, fashion, spiced and flavored with real full-blood aristocracy from all parts of the Union and the old world—all mingling unrestrainedly, and, like a garden of flowers, each swaying in obedience to its own beautiful instinct—that woman assumes her highest form of development, and puts on all her powers of fascina-

7*

tion and display. In home circles in large cities, a kind of conventional barrier is erected around a fashionable woman, which she seldom masters courage to overleap; but where everybody comes and goes in a month, and memory will not stoop to record the flirtings and coquettings of the hour, there is no time to build up these artificial fences, and no material of which to compose them. The drawing-rooms and the broad halls of the hotel become an unobstructed area for the display of every whim or caprice born in a pretty woman's brain, like bubbles in the bright champagne—a race-course for every folly to enter and run its career unimpeded.

After making a fashionable toilette, breakfast is the next important event—and this is loitered over as long as possible, listening to proposals for the morning walk, the afternoon drive, or the evening *hop*-eration, and digest simultaneously scandal and scrambled eggs—a stroll to Chartres street, to patronize those fashionable *modistes*, Olympic and Scanlan, where are found the most exquisite material for ball dresses, the most superb laces, embroideries and artificial flowers on this side of the Atlantic.

At dinner takes place the grand daylight display.

Here it is that the ambition, the ostentation, the panting struggle for superiority in mere external appearance, which is the essence of the life of a fashionable woman, is displayed. The labor expended by Thomson upon his "Seasons," Powers on his statues, or Longfellow on his poems, which startle and illuminate the world, is all surpassed by the pains of care, the agonies of anxiety, lavished by the fashionable woman upon her *costume de diner*. It is here the perfection of art, the highest effect of human shrewdness, in fact, the loftiest result of feminine genius written in velvets, silks, laces and ribbons, becomes resplendently apparent; and when the various fabrics and products of art are used sparingly and discreetly, to heighten and bring out the effects of a woman's natural charms and gifts of person, dress rises to the dignity of an art, and becomes the worthy object of the employment and the ambition of those only natural artists, the women. You can not deny that it is dazzling, if you are forced to confess it is folly.

In this magnificent hotel are located for the season, Mrs. M—— of Kentucky, the widow of Judge J. J. M——. She has been for many years a presiding genius of fashion and society, a lady of great cultivation and conversational powers. We have the handsome and world-renowned Mrs. General G——, and her amiable daughter. The pleasing and distinguished Mrs. M——, Mrs. P——, and the pretty Mrs. H——, of New York, Mrs. Colonel L——, of Louisiana, who is the embodiment of elegance, grace and accomplishments, and also her sweet daughter, who is the reigning belle of the season. Their presence amidst the gayeties of the Saint Charles will throw an unwonted charm and fascination over the whole scene.

On the 17th ultimo the Supreme Court of Louisiana decided the celebrated case of that heroic and admirable lady, Mrs. General Gaines, in her favor. The last will of the once lordly Daniel Clark, charged to have been destroyed—the will of 1813, recognizing the legitimacy of Myra Clark Gaines, has been ordered by the court of last resort, in this State, to be admitted to probate and executed. The effect of this decision will be to give Mrs. Gaines the title to one of the largest estates in this country—an estate of millions. I know of no one into whose hands such vast possessions could be placed· who could use them with a nicer judgment. The unparalleled zeal and earnestness with which this amiable lady has prosecuted her claim has not been prompted by a desire for money, a love for power and fortune; her pure and noble heart wished to vindicate the sacredness of her origin—to establish her *status*—to redeem the fair fame of those to whom she owed her existence. This attainment cheered the dark hours of her affliction, and supported her under many oppressive disappointments and rebuffs. Procrastination, so fatal to sanguine hearts, had no violent dread for her noble spirit. Feeling the justness of her claim, she arose from every disappointment with renewed hope, life, and vigor. With a faith almost amounting to reality, she expended her fortunes, her energies, the vigor of her mind, the best years of life, prosecuting her claim, displaying a perseverance, constancy and fortitude, which justly entitle her to rank among the heroines of history. The persecution of her enemies in her ceaseless toil in prosecuting this complicated litigation, would have appalled a sterner heart. She has surmounted all in honor. The devotion of this noble, spirited women, amidst all her trials, never lessened towards her husband and children. To know Mrs. Gaines is to love and admire her. She has carried her misfortune, as few know how to carry their fortunes, with cheerfulness and moderation.

The new custom house, New Orleans, in process of erection, was commenced October 23, 1848, the plan of Mr. A. T. Wood, architect, having been adopted November 22, 1847, by the Hon. Robert J. Walker, Secretary of the Treasury. The form of this building is a trapezium of 87,333 square feet, or about two acres, being about 30,000 feet greater than the Capitol at Washington without the extension. The four fronts are faced with granite ashlar, plain and massive in style, alike in distribution, and of about the following dimensions:

Canal street front......................	334	feet.
Old Levee............................	196	"
New Levee...........................	310	"
Custom House street..................	251	"

and averaging about eighty-five feet in height. The floors of the second and third stories are carried by massive joined arches of brick, most carefully executed. The fourth floor will be of iron, and also the roof. In the center of the building will be the collector's room, one hundred and sixteen feet by ninety, of pure white marble, with an anterior peristyle of fourteen marble columns and double-faced entablatures, from the fine example of the Choragic monument of Lysicrates. The whole will be surmounted by a dome and lantern, rising to the height of one hundred and thirty feet. The building, when completed, will contain within its ample area, five apartments for the post office, United States courts and land offices, in addition to the offices and all the storage room required for the collection of the revenue at this port; and it may be remarked that several magnificent apartments in the basement and second stories have already been turned over to the appraisers of the customs, affording the amplest facilities for that branch of the service. The building has already cost about one and a half millions of dollars, and another million will probably complete it, in about two and a half to three years. The force varies according to the amount of material received from contractors; from one hundred to two hundred hands are employed, and no pains have been spared by the present commissioners, A. G. Penn and Major G. T. Beauregard, sustained by the Hon. James Guthrie, Secretary of the Treasury, in expediting the completion of this largest and most perfectly arranged structure ever assigned in this country to the revenue service.

I notice, with no ordinary feelings of gratification, they have here an admirable system of common or free school education, far superior to that of many of the other southern States. The public exhibition of the high school graduating classes, which came off last week in Lyceum Hall, did much credit to all engaged in this system of school education. The subjects for composition were well chosen, written and delivered in a style which would have done honor to those of riper years. I have not room in this letter for detail, but I would remark the one by Alfred W. P., "The Resources of the South," and "The Progress of Science," by Miss. Fannie E., and also "The Uses of Knowledge," by Miss Eliza B., were compositions worthy highly intellectual minds. I am glad that Louisiana has set, in this most important question, an example for her sister States.

XXII.

Down the Mississippi.—New Orleans.—A Bal Masque.

STEAMER MAGNOLIA, MISSISSIPPI RIVER, February, 1856.

THE steam is up, the bell has rung, and I am again sailing down the Mississippi on one of those fine packets of the lower trade. These surpass most of the Louisville boats, which are much finer and more comfortable than most boats we have North. The day is lovely, and the magnificent steamer sweeps the water of this noble stream with a grace and dignity to inspire one with the belief that she is the queen of steamers. A soft, lively wind is blowing from the south, and every thing is swaying about lazily and peacefully in the breeze, while the blue sky, mottled with soft white clouds, bends down and smiles lovingly from above. My *compagnons de voyage* seem kind, sociable, and obliging, and have all the affability of well-bred southerners. A more cheerful tone of feeling pervades the saloon. There is more deference paid to ladies among southern travelers than among northern. Southerners are a warm-hearted people, and study the comfort of others, which is the only true politeness. At the North speculation seems to have become an institution of the land. In ordinary intercourse of meeting strangers it is observable. A northern traveler seems absorbed in thought, calculating on the next election, his banking or commercial pursuits, and too often forgets the courtesies due to fellow-travelers, though in society and among friends they are a polite and well-bred people.

I have just descended from the deck, where I have been to promenade for exercise, and had the pleasure of watching a real Claude sunset, from its glow to its death-shroud. It was a pure southern sunset, with all its characteristics—its harmony, its grandeur, its loveliness. We were surrounded on either side by immense plantations, and the eye strayed over their vast expanse. There were the dark blue distance, and the deep blue sky; and the last beam of its setting smile was playing upon the walls of the neighboring mansions and forming rainbow pictures in the broad stream below. The purple and gold of the "dying dolphin" lay soft and languid upon the distant wood; and as I gazed upon this glory, I involuntarily exclaimed, "How beautiful!" I have seen many rich and varied sunsets at the North, on our lakes and among our mountains: they are much more brilliant, and have bolder, more confused, unsettled and varied coloring, but they want that soft misty vail which gives to the southern sunset its depth, its languor, its repose.

Captain Thomason, master of this well-known and favorite steamer, has just entered the ladies' saloon. He bows gracefully, and pays his respects to Mrs. Prewett, editress of the *Yazoo Banner*, a lady who displays a fund of cleverness, of common sense, of practical business-like habits. I am told her journal rendered its party great service in the last fall's campaign.

Sunday, 24.—Our dinner to-day was a sumptuous affair, served in great elegance and taste. Captain Thomason is as *au fait* as a master of ceremonies at his table, as he is skillful in command; and if one wishes to realize the pleasure of steaming on the Mississippi, they should make a trip on the Magnolia.

Monday, 25.—We arrived in New Orleans before sunrise. It is a delightful morning. Mingled with the immense shipping of this port lay scattered around us, and gliding in gracefully at every passway, barges and boats freighted with all the tropical fruits and magnificent shells, arranged in the most picturesque order, which the boatmen, in red caps, offer, in French, Spanish, and bad English, for sale to travelers. The wharf seems a mountain of cotton bales.

I have driven to the Saint Charles. Not a vacant room in the house. Fifty persons waiting in the reception-room, who have hurried up from the boats and railway, relying upon the old adage, "First come, first served." My chance seems rather a slim one, not making the first scramble. However, the agreeable landlord says if I will wait until night he will try and find me a place, and with that promise no one ever leaves this house. I never before saw such a crowd of gayety and fashion in one house. I am informed on good authority that the proprietors of this excellent hotel have realized as a profit a thousand dollars per day for the last three months; but how they manage to make every one so comfortable and happy in this great caravansery of fashion I can't imagine.

All who love society, pleasure and comfort never fail in winter to pass a few weeks in New Orleans. The majority go to this house; and I am not surprised that the Saint Charles has become so widely known, and always well filled under its able management, although two other first-class hotels are in the city.

Tuesday morning, 26.—The city is unusually healthy—weather charming, and business brisk. A masked ball came off at the Saint Louis last night. I am told it was well attended. One of my New York friends tells me he was dreadfully quizzed, and can't imagine who the taunting witch was. Bal Masque is racy, grand and brilliant. Amicability reigns supreme. "Give and take" is the motto. A hasty "pardon" is sufficient atonement for a ruined chapeau, a torn robe or a stolen mouchoir.

At this house last night we had a hop. The ladies were dressed charmingly. There is no place, save Paris, where ball dresses are so exquisitely beautiful as here. There is not that great struggle for preëminence at fashionable gatherings here as at the North. The spirit of exclusiveness, so paralyzing in its influence, which makes everybody so uncomfortable, and half neutralizes the pleasure of a sojourn at a fashionable place, is never experienced in well-bred society South.

XXIII.

Vicksburg.—Mississippi Steamboats.

WASHINGTON HOTEL, VICKSBURG, March 14, 1856.

THE day is delightful, weather perfect, and the first pleasant one since I reached here. I leave to-day for Memphis, waiting for the Ingomar, one of the New Orleans and Memphis packets. She was due here last evening, but owing to the heavy fogs on the river, the boats at night are often detained for hours, and sometimes the whole night. The weather has been so unfavorable during my stay here I have seen but little of the city. It is a place of enterprise and business, and the location one of the prettiest on the river. It is situated upon a high bluff, having many terraced walks, and grounds fringed with shade trees, and squares filled with shrubbery and beautiful flowers, and for some distance around the country is dotted over with neat and handsome mansions. The city has many fine churches and edifices of a good deal of architectural taste and beauty. When the railroads are completed which are to center here, Vicksburg will advance more rapidly than at present. No city of her population can boast of better accommodations for strangers. She supports two large, well-managed, first-class hotels, one of which, the Washington Hotel, for comfort, convenience and neatness, is not surpassed by any. It is under the able management of General McMackin, whose kind, benevolent smile, and polite attentions, make all his guests feel at home. His table is a sumptuous one, and the waiters are innumerable, and the best trained, I have met South.

Two or three blocks from the hotel, which is but one from the river, the view of the country and river, for sixty miles around, or as far as the eye can reach, is peerless, and the water to-day is sparkling with sunbeams. Boats built for use display only ease and grace in form and motion. The opposite shore is Louisiana, and presents to the eye an expanse of low, flat ground. I am told, from Baton Rouge to Memphis, a distance of six hundred and fifty miles, on either side of the river, is the finest cotton region in the United States. The income of many a planter in this section, from his cotton alone, is eighty or a hundred thousand dollars per year. Many of them live in magnificent style, visit New Orleans every winter, where they pass two or three months in gayety and fashion, and, I assure you, I think there is no place in this country where they could kill time more agreeably.

The Vicksburg, Shreveport and Texas Railroad is opposite this place. The country which will become tributary to this road when finished has suffered a loss, I am told, in consequence of inaccessibility to market. That portion of the road lying between Vicksburg and Monroe crosses a body of bottom lands second to none in the world of the same extent for capability of producing fine staple cotton. Most of those lands, it is said, are almost valueless for the want of an outlet to market. The whole of the north of Louisiana will be made accessible to emigrants from the old States, and, west of Red river, it reaches out to grasp the immense trade of Texas and bring it to the Mississippi. Its geographical position is such as to monopolize at once the entire travel between Texas and the States east of the Mississippi; and to Vicksburg, whose citizens have so nobly contributed to the enterprise, its advantages can not be too highly estimated, as travel must pass through here.

I have just been called to the balcony to look at the steamboat New World, from Arkansas. She is freighted with five thousand bales of cotton; her guards and hurricane deck are perfectly covered, no unusual sight at this season. The Mississippi is navigable twenty-one hundred miles; passing a small portage, three thousand may be achieved. It embraces the productions of many climates.

The upper Mississippi, a mining country, abounds in coal, lead, iron and copper, in veins of wonderful richness; and on the lower Mississippi the climate is favorable to almost all the productions of the tropics. The sugar, the cotton plant, the orange, the lemon, the grape, the banana, the mulberry, tobacco, rice, maize, sweet potato, all flourish in rich abundance, and some of them attain to a luxuriance of growth scarcely known in any other part of the world. Sugar and cotton are the two great staples. The former is confined chiefly to that tract which, by way of distinction, is called "the coast," lying along the shores of the Gulf, and the bayous of the Mississippi.

March 15.—The Ingomar did not reach the wharf until after midnight. We had a pleasant moonlight drive to the river, and going on board found the steamer, which is a large boat, with superior accommodations.

March 16.—The weather is clear and fine, and as warm as the middle of May at the North. The steamer has made a good run to-day, with the exception of a short detention, caused by a big log getting caught in the wheel, when she was obliged to put back two miles and a half, and run ashore to cut it out. The river is now almost covered with drift, still it but slightly impedes navigation. and causes no serious accidents. In the ladies' saloon, last night, we had conversation, music. dancing, and whist. All was conducted in such good taste it seemed more like a party of friends than travelers accidentally thrown together.

I often wish an abolitionist would come South and make a trip on a Mississippi packet, for I think he would acknowledge that the black waiters and attendants on these boats, all of whom are slaves, are the best dressed, the best cared for, and happiest working class he had met; and the servants, too, who are traveling with their masters and mistresses, are invariably neatly and handsomely dressed, and, I may add, look fat and lazy. They go to the second table, and are given every delicacy on it; joke and laugh, and, I assure you, seem very little like the oppressed, down-trodden race they are represented to be by northern abolitionists. The blacks are very communicative, if you give them an oppportunity. I sometimes talk with them, and have often asked them if they would like to be free. They say, "Oh, no! missus, I 's do n't want to be free; massa and missus takes good care of us, and we 's a heap better off than free niggers." This is their general response when interrogated about freedom. So far from the institution being guilty of degrading the negro, and keeping him in degradation, it has elevated him in the scale of being far above his brethren in Africa, and is continuing to do so. I feel that no people have been more misrepresented, and have had more injustice done them than southern slaveholders. We are safely at Memphis. I must close and get ready to go ashore.

XXIV.

Memphis. — Its Banks and Bachelors. — The Ladies. — Worsham House. — Waiting for a Boat. — Miss Murray. — Left. — Off.

WORSHAM HOUSE, MEMPHIS, March 22, 1856.

I REACHED here on the 17th instant. I have seen but little of the city, merely the center, where business has called me. I am told by Mr. D., to whom I brought letters of introduction, that the annual exports from this place (mostly cotton,) are twelve millions a year—that business increases faster than the population, which is about eighteen thousand. This city has appropriated a large fund and has a fine system of free school education. Four railroads are commenced that are to center here. The progress made in the construction of public works in the southern States is slow, and the benefits which every day's experience proves would be conferred on the States by their early completion render the subject, I should think, one of chief importance to their public policy, but they seem to shrink from a vigorous activity amidst the general progress of the nation, and fail to form a just contemplation of their own necessities.

If in railroads and manufactures Memphis is behind the age, she can boast of more banks and bachelors than any other city in the Union of its size. I am told there are twenty bachelors to one young lady, and at least a dozen banks, though there are very few bank bills in circulation that are redeemable here. She maintains five daily newspapers, all edited with ability, and two of which are very sprightly ones. With reading such journals her citizens can but be intelligent.

There are quite a number of pretty ladies here; but in some instances I observe bad taste in costume. They wear too many gay and light colors in street costume, and not always harmoniously arranged, which, instead of heightening and bringing out the effects of a woman's charms and natural gifts of person, detract therefrom. Grave colors are much more elegant and becoming, as well as suitable for street dresses. When the various light and gay-colored fabrics are used in dress, they should be arranged artistically so as not to offend the eye. In dress a lady should cultivate taste, and have genius to adapt her costume to herself and her own peculiar order of beauty. Dressing expensively and magnificently when not tastefully arranged, is a mere barbarian luxury.

Memphis is destined in a few years to be next in a commercial point of view on the Mississippi to St. Louis, and is now a fine city, but without much architectural style in building. It would be a great improvement to the place if her streets were graded and walks better paved. The reason of the delay, I am told, is because they have no material of which to compose them, there being no rock within a hundred miles of the city.

This place supports two large hotels, of which the Worsham House is said to be the best. It is neat, well-appointed and kept—an excellent table, and polite attendance. Mr. Worsham, the landlord, is an agreeable gentleman, and superintends this fine establishment, and is ever on the look-out to make his guests comfortable.

Monday morning, March 24.—I have been waiting, for the last forty-eight hours, in bonnet, mantle, and gloves, for the steamer Niagara to take me up the river. She has just passed, and I am left, although she stopped at the wharf some time. I have expended breath enough, in the last two days, talking to the big black porter, to put me on that boat when she came, and not let me be left, had it been steam, to have brought her up from New Orleans. In a perfect frenzy of disappointment and despair, I am back in my room again, whose walls and appointments now look as gloomy as a hearse in yellow fever time.

Now, Mr. Editor, it is not a very pleasant thing to eat in bonnet and gloves, and sleep in one's chair forty-eight hours, for fear of missing a boat, and hear fifty-nine steamboat whistles a day, gather up a well-filled satchel, extra shawl and book, run down stairs, and when at the foot be told "it ain't your boat"—walk back to your room with a racking headache, sad, gloomy, and weary with disappointment, and waiting to conjugate, like the Great Frederic, the verb "Ennuyer"—or open Miss Murray's book to read, which is dull and uninteresting, and some of its information about as correct as a hotel porter's. However, there 's one thing I admire, the justness with which she speaks of the South and their domestic institutions.

When the Niagara was finally announced, I stepped into the hack in ecstasy and gratitude—feeling on good terms with the whole world—drove one block, and to my great horror saw the boat sailing off with as much grace and complacency as if she had taken every thing on board that wanted to go. Her officers on deck looking independent, and I in despair looking at the huge monster, wishing I had a cable to hold her fast. No use hoisting a flag of distress. I was on land high and dry, and she would n't put back for a tear drowning. When I reproached the porter for his tardiness, the cold-hearted fellow actually smiled; but I believe more in pity than at my disappointment; for he says he sat up all night watching for her, and had fallen asleep at ten this morning when she came. Weather delightful—the sky without a cloud, but time horrible to endure. I have tried every thing—but every thing seems wearisome—reading is a bore—writing is laborious—the desire to proceed—the certainty of delay, all tend to create an irritability of temper if any woman could resist, would deserve the name of Angel-ina. I'll tell you what it is, I'll send for the porter and give him a fresh set of orders—turn stoic and philosopher, and go to sleep if I can

—no water craft whistle shall disturb my nerves for the next twelve hours.

Tuesday evening, March 25.—After a refreshing night's sleep and an idle day, I am on board the Tishamingo, bound for Louisville. She is a fine steamer, full of passengers, and her master, Captain Baiscoe, has the reputation of a careful and skillful commander. Mr. Levi, her clerk, is a gentleman whose kind and benevolent smile makes all the wayfarers feel quite at ease about comfort and safety, and every thing bespeaks a pleasant trip.

XXV.

Nashville.—The State Capitol.—University of Nashville.—The Hume High School.—City Hotel.

City Hotel, Nashville, April 11, 1856.

Nashville is located upon a rocky site—an eminence, some points of which rise two hundred feet above the level of the Cumberland river. The scenery surrounding it is very beautiful, watered by a river capable of floating steamers of medium size, winding through the valley, or making its way through red sand-stone hills, to which must be added the rich and varied foliage of the South. The streets are finely graded, and the walks handsomely flagged in the vicinity of the private residences; but in some of the principal business streets it is the reverse, for which, by the way, there is no excuse, with a superfluous abundance of material within half a mile of the city. Another fault I observe is a bad system of drainage. Slops are thrown into the alleys, and, without any excuse, there suffered to remain; for, besides the descent to the river, I am told there are no less than three caves under the city, one of which underlies a portion of the center, and has its mouth on the river bluff. This could be made available by introducing a sewer into it, and, I would imagine, comparatively speaking, at small expense. They have as yet but one railroad completed, the Chatanooga, of which the freight-house and buildings at the dépôt are fine.

If in some things Nashville may be called "old fogy," and a little behind the age, she can boast of the finest State capitol, now nearly finished, in the Union. The site of this building could not be more beautiful. Imagine a hill in the center of a city, rising two hundred feet above the level of the Cumberland river, at this place, four feet of its crest being removed, leaving a plateau of solid limestone for the foundation of the building. At your feet you overlook the city, and the view beyond is bounded on all sides by a far distant amphitheater of mountain ranges.

It is of the Grecian order of architecture, consisting of a Doric basement, supporting on its four fronts porticoes of the Ionic order. The structure is composed of fossilated and beautifully-variegated limestone, hewn and chiseled from quarries in the neighborhood of Nashville. In the center and above the roof, rises a tower to the height of eighty-one feet, the superstructure of which is after the order of the Choragic monument of Lysicrates, at Athens. The ceilings are arched throughout, and, I am told, the halls and chambers are pleasant to speak in, and excellent for sound. The laws of acoustics can not be too carefully studied in constructing public edifices. The rafters are of wrought iron, supported by interior walls, the whole covered with thick sheets of copper. A cast iron stairway leads from the roof to the top of the tower, which is intended, when finished, for an observatory.

The hall of the Representatives contains sixteen fluted columns of the Roman Ionic order, two feet eight inches in diameter, and twenty-one feet ten inches in height. The shafts or columns of these are all in one piece. The forum of the House of Representatives consists of a semicircular platform, three feet in height, forming three steps, upon which there is a screen of East Tennessee marble, surmounted by an eagle resting upon a shield of cast iron, bronzed and gilt. One foot from each end of the screen, on a die of black marble, the Roman fasces are placed, which are of beautifully-variegated East Tennessee marble.

The Senate chamber is of an oblong form, having pilasters of the Ionic order, with a full entablature. The ceilings of this room are formed into radiating panels. There is a gallery on three sides of the room, supported by twelve columns of variegated East Tennessee marble, with white capitals and black bases, from the Erectheum. The forum in this room consists of a platform of two steps. The speaker's and clerk's desks are of fine East Tennessee marble.

The doors and windows, which are of a large size, are all of solid white oak, molded, paneled and ornamented with devices. The windows are all double, divided by stone pilasters, enriched with consoles, ovolo and spears. The glass is of a superior quality, and was made at the works near Knoxville, East Tennessee. I am told all of the materials of which this magnificent structure is composed were furnished by the State of Tennessee. All the floors are grain-arched, and flagged with rubbed stone. Hanging stone steps throughout the building. The building is in the form of a parallelogram, surrounded by a terrace flagged with stone, with flights of steps in the center of each front, opposite the doors of entrance. Twenty-eight fluted columns, four feet eight inches in diameter, ornamenting the four porticoes, with most elaborate wrought capitals. The north and south porticoes are finished with pediments, containing ceilings of stone, and the east and west porticoes are surmounted by parapets. Those of the north and south are octo style and those of the east and west hepas style. Francis W. Strickland, the architect, has immortalized his name with the masterly skill and fine taste which he has displayed in the design and finish of this magnificent building. The grounds are extensive; and when laid out, and ornamented with shrubbery and flowers, this will be the most beautiful place in this country.

I visited the Western Military Institute, now the collegiate department of the University of Nashville, and had the pleasure of making the acquaintance of that agreeable and highly scientific gentleman, Lieutenant Colonel Richard Owen, commandant and professor of geology and chemistry in this Institute.

The Western Military Institute, incorporated in

the State of Kentucky in 1847, and erected at Drennon Springs, during seven years enjoyed in that State a very extensive patronage. In 1853, with two hundred and thirty students in attendance, and in public favor through the South and West, they found it necessary, on account of unusual sickness, to disband the students. A temporary location was made at Tyree Springs, in this State. In 1854 it accepted articles of union with the University of Nashville, and is now the collegiate or literary department of that institute.

The institute has already passed successfully through its first session at Nashville, with one hundred and twenty matriculants, and the half session just opened indicates the probability of a considerable increase.

The number of volumes in the libraries of the university is about fourteen thousand; it has also a chemical apparatus, a handsome cabinet of minerals, fossils and other specimens of natural history, arranged in the most scientific and perfect order by Professor Owen, with casts, maps and diagrams, and a good collection of mathematical and philosophical instruments, which afford superior facilities to the student in the elucidation of the princi-

ples of several branches of science. Their method of teaching is a most excellent one, all that is possible being presented to the mind through the eye.

The collegiate department is located upon a lovely site, with extensive grounds, about a mile from the city. The buildings consist of a magnificent stone edifice, an imposing brick building three stories high, of a style of architecture in harmony with the stone edifice, and a large brick building for the accommodation of professors and their families, with a wing attached one hundred and thirty-two feet long, containing dining hall, kitchen, laundry, store and shops for the accommodation of professors and students. As a whole, I am much pleased with this institute. At present, Professor Owen is laying out on the college grounds a geological garden, which is to represent, geographically, both the mineral and vegetable productions of each State in the Union. It will be the means of affording amusement and great instruction to the students.

Parents in this country, where there is a great lack of athletic exercises, would, in educating their sons, find it to their advantage to have superadded to the collegiate course, military instruction, yet I would not recommend it so much for the present organization, as the personal, physical, and moral advantages attained by military exercise and military discipline. Compared with the military drill, no system of physical training ever devised is better adapted to the student. It takes him from his books, over which he has been bending for hours, brings him to an erect position, gives him a firm, graceful, manly carriage, expands his chest, puts into harmonious action every limb and muscle, and thus promotes a perfect physical development, and a consequent increase of mental vigor, and also promotes three great moral principles—obedience, subordination, and method.

A few years since the corporate authorities of Nashville established a public school, free to all residing in the corporate limits. It is called Hume High School, to perpetuate the memory of a celebrated teacher of that name, lately deceased. I am told the school is in a most prosperous condition, provided with the very best teachers, and the hearts of thousands of the recipients are already made glad and grateful for this great blessing.

In traveling over this whole extent of country, I

have seldom, if ever, found better or more superior accommodation for strangers than at the City Hotel. Comfortable apartments, well ventilated; prompt attention from polite and well-drilled servants; and a table bountifully supplied with good things—substantials, varieties, and delicacies, that this fine surrounding country about Nashville affords. No more agreeable gentlemen, and kind host, can anywhere be found than Mr. Scott, the proprietor, and his superintendent, Mr. Foss, formerly of New York, a gentleman of superior education and intelligence. They receive strangers with such polite, easy and fine manners as to make them feel at once they are in a superior house. I take pleasure in commending this house to strangers visiting Nashville, and feel sure all who go there will find true what I have said in its favor.

This city has many handsome private residences tastefully furnished, some in sumptuous and magnificent style, and all surrounded by beautifully laid out grounds which give them a look of retirement and repose, and they are more like the splendid palaces of opulence and rank, surrounded by the gardens of fashion, than the habitations of a republican city. Those persons I had the pleasure of meeting were highly educated and intelligent, and many very accomplished. I made the acquaintance of Mrs. Frances B. Fogg, who is at the head of the literary and fashionable coteries of Nashville, and also an authoress, possessing rare accomplishments and the best qualities of heart and mind, combined with a joyous and genial disposition, and no one can approach her without feeling it.

Saturday, April 12.—I am again on my way to Louisville, on board the "Rock City," a Nashville and Paducah packet. She is a fine boat. Captain Egan, her commander, a pleasant gentleman; and we have a fair prospect of a fine sail to the mouth of the river, where we must reship for Louisville.

The two past days have been oppressively hot in Nashville, with a wind blowing almost a simoom, bearing upon its wings clouds of dust, much to the discomfiture of pedestrians. A flash of lightning, a roll of thunder, and the big rain-drops are pouring on the deck. The cloud-capped hills are perfectly lighted up by the electric chain; the hoarse thunder re-echoes in every valley. It is one of those scenes which, being of God himself, alone deserves the epithets of grandeur and sublimity that ambitious man is so prone to heap upon the insignificant and filagree nothingness that he calls the evidences of his creative genius. The breathing statue, the glowing canvas, the gorgeous temple, what are they all compared to the inexhaustible sea of light streaming upon us from yon clouds, hung like dark curtains over the heavens, as if to shut out from mortal eyes the holy mysteries of the hour!

The celestial scene has passed, and the clouds, bleached of their dark and flaming hues, are fading behind the invisible curtains of the air. The moon, just rounded to the full outline of her beauty, is slowly creeping up from the east, her sweet face and silvery light are partially vailed by a soft cloud crossing her path. The stars are coming out in many clusters to wink and sparkle. Diana, in her most dazzling light, with the little dim-eyed creatures that ever wait submissive at her side. Good night. The thousands of wondering faces which have been mutely upturned to heaven to witness the magnificent scene, must now seek their pillows and their dreams, and the noiseless universe will go its way.

Monday, April 14.—Yesterday we were fortu-

nate in meeting at Smithland, and reshipped without delay to the steamer Niagara, the identical boat that left me with such *nonchalance* at Memphis a few weeks since. I can not close without paying a well merited eulogy to this boat. Heretofore, I have had a dislike to steamboat traveling, my impressions arising from experience on northern boats, which are smaller, and accommodations much inferior to southern ones. Imagine an immense boat, neat as a quaker household, with a succession of saloons, furnished in the most luxurious style; state rooms with all the comforts and appointments of a home chamber; tables arranged width-wise the saloon, suitable for a party of a dozen, set with rich plate, crystal, and china, and furnished with the most sumptuous fare—all the appetizing luxuries that can be purchased in the markets of New Orleans and Louisville, cooked and served in perfect order and elegance. Breakfast served from seven to ten o'clock; dinner, from two to four; tea at six; and supper at any time during the night; and you will have a fair picture and some idea of the steamer Niagara. Captain Spotts, in his skillful command, has won an enviable reputation. Captain Charles F. Reynolds, the chief clerk is a Kentuckian, and possesses in a high degree the fine qualities of the Kentucky gentleman. Mr. Barclay, his assistant, is a gallant young man, of kind and obliging manners.

XXVI.

Raining Down at Night in New York—The Saint Nicholas Hotel.—Its Extent and Magnificence.

ST. NICHOLAS HOTEL, NEW YORK, May 26, 1856.

WELL, here I am at last, and after drawing a very long breath, I sit down to inform you of my safe arrival. Did you or any of your readers, by the way, ever reach New York at twelve o'clock at night, and in a rain storm? Well, I *have*—I know the beauties of the scene, and *some* of its more hideous aspects. Just imagine a woman, shaken all day on the Harlem railroad, arriving in this city of mud, misery, and magnificence, at midnight, with no attendant—the skies dark, gloomy, forbidding, and constantly pouring down upon the devoted pavement such a torrent of rain as is only known in June showers. Then drive to one hotel, and be told by the surly clerk, as he rubs his eyes in amazement to see a "lone female" at that hour of the night requesting shelter—"all full." Then try another, with the same result. A third, and ditto;

and finally resolve, in a fit of desperation, to go to the biggest house in town, the place where it is said they can accommodate the Congress of the United States, the Parliament of England, the Assemblies of France, &c., &c., &c. This I did, and happy was I in being allowed to rest my weary body. All honor, I say, to a hotel that does not get *full.*

I have been thinking what a journey I have had, to be sure. Let me see—I have been in twelve different States since last December, and visited the cities of Louisville, Frankfort, Lexington, Nashville, Memphis, Natchez, Baton Rouge, New Orleans, Montgomery, Mobile, Jackson, and St. Louis, to say nothing of other places nearer home. The Mississippi river has become almost as familiar as the pretty little brook in the country on whose banks, in the sunny hours of childhood, I used to gather the violet and the lily. There is no danger, however, of my ever mistaking the one for the other. The banks of the country stream, perfumed with its verdant borders of "brookmint," bear no resemblance to the turbid river which rolls its wealth of waters so majestically along, creating, as it were, just for its own spiteful amusement, sand-bars and snags wherewith to try the patience of those who navigate it. But southerners *have* patience. Did you ever think of that fact? Why, northerners could no more get along with the negroes of the South than they could make one.

Of all the dumbest, inefficient *humans* in the world, I will set up negroes as the cap-sheaf. They are essentially children. For instance, I would tell the servant, when stopping at a hotel, that I wanted such or such a thing done at a particular time. But it was useless; she never did it. There is no use of telling *me* that the negroes have no incitement to work. They would not work if they were free *at all*, but live on herbs and snakes, as they do in Africa. As for educating them, with the exception of those who are mulattoes, and thus have more or less white blood, you might as well educate an ox, expecting to make a horse of him by the process, as to educate a negro, expecting you will make him a white man. My idea is, if he had ever been intended to occupy the position of a white man he would never have been made *black*, and that is as far as I care about arguing the question with anybody.

Since I returned, I have been looking around, and I have come to the *unanimous* conclusion that, after all, New York is the greatest city on this continent, and bound to be a still greater one; and, what is more, has the greatest hotel. I had often been in the parlors of the St. Nicholas in calling upon friends in town, but had never before my raining down here the other night been any further initiated into this labyrinthian establishment. Since then, I have been "investigating," and I must say, that for sumptuous magnificence and profuse though not gaudy decorations, I have never seen its equal. Its proportions are so gigantic that the mind hesitates at first to be awed by its effect, not being willing that this sentiment, which only responds to the grand, should be stirred into activity by a hotel. But when one wanders through its long halls, ascends its stairs, treads miniature streets, descends another flight, again pursues his way, turns to the right and sees rows of doors duly numbered, turns to the left and beholds the same, follows on to see the end of this puzzle, again ascends to another floor, finds still no end, the doors now numbering somewhere away up among the hundreds, he comes down again to the first floor, sits down and exclaims, "Immense!"

Besides, however, the size of this house, which, of course, surpasses any thing on this continent, and, indeed, in the world, the system and management is, after all, the most important point. Mr. Rodgers, the superintendent, who attends to the details of the establishment, seems to be one of those quiet, semi-omnipresent beings who is all over. Go into the parlor, he is there; into the tea room, he is there; in the dining room, he is there; in fact, Mr. Rodgers, like the man in the play, pops up where least expected, but when wanted the most. Some twelve hundred people can be comfortably accommodated in this prodigious hotel. But if there be one thing more than another in which it surpasses even itself, it is in its *table de hote.* Gastronomy is here carried to the perfection that it was among the Romans, whose *cuisnes,* we are told, could so cook pork as to make the most experienced devotee of Bacchus believe he was eating chicken. The dining rooms sparkle and shine with the light reflected from the most expensive chandeliers, the elegant china on the tables, the beautifully frescoed walls, the flashing of all the tints of the rainbow from the thousand articles of cut glass, lends a beauty and harmony to the scene as enchanting as the fairy palace of Calypso, which beguiled the youthful Telemachus from his patriotic and filial duties.

But modern magnificence far surpasses all that the ignorant old Greeks or Romans ever dreamed of. They never thought of gas streaming from a thousand burners, of entire palaces heated by some conquered volcano, whose eternal fire has been made subservient to man; and of lightning telegraphs, which "speak and it is done." No; these wonders have been left for the nineteenth century, and the guests of the Saint Nicholas. And yet this house is to be improved! A space has been procured in Mercer street, and ninety new rooms are to be added! Americans may go to English hotels to get surly looks and unsociable manners, to French hotels to live on frogs and pastry, to German hotels to be smothered between prodigious feather beds, and to Italian hotels to be robbed by waiters and employees, but in all their travels they will never come across so obliging, so convenient, so well arranged an establishment as their national institution, the Saint Nicholas.

There is only one more advantage it could possibly enjoy to render it the most luxurious and enticing place on the continent of America; that is, the soft, balmy, tropical atmosphere of New Orleans in December. Let the fragrance of orange groves and the scent of the banana be mingled with the mild breath of the tropics, and it produces an enchanting atmosphere, in which the displays of magnificence are set off to double advantage. The ladies here are coming out in their summer dresses, but I can not generally praise their taste. There is great richness and variety of attire; but too often real elegance is sacrificed to gaudy display, as if the art of dressing consisted in the quantity of furbelows and flounces. Elegance of dress is neatness without ostentation, richness without profusion, and appropriateness without affectation.

XXVII.

Politics in Illinois.—Prospects of Chicago.—New Buildings, &c.

BRIGGS HOUSE, CHICAGO, July 2, 1856.

IN this State, the political cauldron already begins to boil. The municipal election in Chicago was most strenuously and powerfully contested. Being the home of Douglas, every effort was made by his enemies to prostrate his influence and defeat his friends; but the exertions of the combined opposition were in vain. Honorable Thomas Dyer, nominated by the democracy for mayor, on a platform at once liberal and anti-sectional, was elected by a large and decisive majority. It was a blow from which the Freesoil Know Nothing fusionists can never recover. The nominations of the Cincinnati Convention are received with enthusiasm in the Prairie State. The wisdom and patriotism of the convention will be amply complimented at the presidential election. No section of the country is truer to the Union and the Constitution than the mighty and illimitable West.

It is admitted, generally, that Richardson will beat Bissell, for governor, from three to five thousand; some of them, however, pretending to think there is a chance for the latter, and that the contest will be very close. The friends of Richardson are sanguine and confident, none claiming less than twenty or thirty thousand majority. From what I hear from the several counties in this State, it is more than probable that the entire ticket, from Colonel Richardson down, will be triumphantly elected. It is predicted, by those who have opportunities of judging, the canvass will be warm and exciting throughout the north end and middle portions of the State; and a great change will be had from that of the last two years, and at least seven or eight of the next Congressmen will be national men, in favor of the Nebraska Bill and the Constitution. In one third of the counties of the State, it will be one-sided—all for Buchanan and Breckinridge, Richardson and Hamilton.

This magic city of the West has trebled its population in the last half dozen years, and claims now to be ninety thousand, and its march is still on.

ward. Much as has been said of the rapid growth of this city, extravagant as have seemed the predictions heretofore ventured respecting her destiny, last year's satistics, I am told, show that the reality far exceeds in magnitude the seemingly most wild conjectures that have ever yet been indulged in respecting her. No doubt Chicago is the greatest primary grain port in the world; and next to the grain trade, that in lumber claims preëminence, and maintains a most powerful rivalry. This important arm of the prosperity of the manufactures of Chicago continues to keep pace with the general growth of the city and country, and is destined to become a great manufacturing center; the wants and capacities of the country with which she is commercially connected demand it. Her system of railroads traverse a region unsurpassed in agricultural resources; and while they offer facilities for transporting the productions of her workshops and factories to those who will use them, they also supply the means for bringing hither the raw material required for their production.

My first visit to Chicago was in the fall of 1854, not two years since, and the apparent progress of commercial and manufacturing interests is not greater than those of city improvements. The character and style of new buildings have altogether changed. Residences have been constructed on a scale of substantial magnificence known in but few cities west of New York, and where then stood buildings decayed and dilapidated, are now to be seen immense store-houses, granaries, and blocks of stores, built in a style of permanence and durability, suggestive of the confidence capitalists have in the future greatness of Chicago. There is also a great improvement in the residences that grace some of the avenues and squares. The "Bishop's Palace," as it is called, is a princely residence. It is beautifully situated on the corner of Michigan avenue and Madison street, and is built of Athens marble. Its architectural proportions are grand and symmetrical; four stories high, has two fronts and two entrances of a most spacious character. It is the residence of Rt. Rev. Dr. O'Regan, and few residences in the United States surpass it.

The Court House in Chicago is a fine structure, built of blue limestone, and of the Doric order, though without columns, and standing in the center of a handsome square, inclosed by a substantial iron railing, and the grounds prettily ornamented with fountains, shade trees and shrubbery. Chicagó is well supplied with material for building. A few feet from the surface the ground yields a fair quality of clay, the lake shore supplies any quantity of sand, and, at reasonable price, can be obtained the drab-colored Milwaukie brick, which, in beauty and durability, yields to no other. But a much more elegant material than the latter is found in great abundance, about twenty miles from the city, on the line of the Illinois canal. It is a limestone of a pale yellow shade, somewhat lighter than the Caen stone now so much sought after for building material in New York. The grain is fine, it is durable and easily wrought, and the color is peculiarly pleasing to the eye, and a more beautiful material for building purposes I have never seen.

Both carriage way and sidewalks are planked. There are a few blocks where the planks have been removed and replaced with broad flag stones. The sidewalks of Chicago are peculiar—a continual succession of ups and downs. With almost every block of buildings there is a change of grade from one foot to five. These ascents and descents are made by steps or inclined planes. The reason of this diversity is, that it was found necessary to raise

the grade of the streets, and as each building is erected, its foundation, and the sidewalk adjoining have been made to correspond to the grade there last established.

Chicago is well supplied with fine, pure water from Lake Michigan. At present this city is remarkably healthy. It is constantly fanned by pure breezes from the lake, a breeze that never sleeps, sweeping over hundreds of miles; and with an efficient system of sewerage from lake to river, Chicago will be one of the healthiest cities in the Union. The Commissioners of Sewerage have been receiving plans from engineers and others as to the best place for building sewers in this city, and the one they have decided on is now before the Common Council for consideration.

This city maintains a great number of hotels, and they are not only well filled but always running over; one of which, the Briggs House, for comfort, convenience, and neatness, is not surpassed by any. There is now being added an addition of eighty rooms, and when completed, it will be one of the largest hotels in Chicago. The first thought and desire of every traveler, on reaching a strange place, is to find a well-kept hotel, one where his every comfort is cared for. I take pleasure in paying a well-merited compliment to the Briggs House, which is under the able management of Messrs. Floyd & French. Its location is good, tables profusely furnished, rooms are large and well appointed, and the house possesses all the modern improvements of eastern hotels. The Tremont still retains its popularity as a first-class hotel; and a new one, the Metropolitan, was opened a week since by the late proprietor of the "City Hotel," of Hartford, Connecticut. It is a fine building, and with the able management of such men it can not but do well.

XXVIII.

In New York Again.—Genin's Bazaar.

ST. NICHOLAS HOTEL, August 25, 1856.

WEARY, worn, and exhausted with traveling, never did sojourner seek the wayside inn with more satisfaction than I my old and comfortable quarters at the St. Nicholas, a few days since, upon my return from the far West. I have long been lost (mayhap satisfactorily) to your readers, but I can not consent to stay lost. Sometimes I think of the DAY BOOK as it *is* and as it *was*, even a year ago—then almost unknown, now an "institution." *Twenty-five thousand subscribers in a single year!* Was the like ever known before? I think not. With your present large and constantly increasing circulation, you must soon become a power in the land. And here permit me to say that New Yorkers are the most obstinate people I know. In the country, South and West, everybody sees, knows and reads the WEEKLY DAY BOOK; here, if I want a copy of your daily, I can't find it! What is the matter? I suspect the people here only read those papers which puff one another.

To change the subject:—New York is as noisy as when I left it last spring, and the St. Nicholas just as large and just as full of people. I find here a number of my southern friends, whose delightful acquaintance I made last winter at the South; indeed, the hotel is now very liberally supplied with people from that much-abused section of the Union. Here they cluster, for they probably find it, like the St. Charles, of New Orleans, the most fascinating of hotels—full of that fashion and *abandon* which give a spice and flavor to existence not elsewhere to be met with. Say what you will, an air of elegance and refinement produces a captivating influence which attracts thousands, and extorts praise and admiration from all who come within the circle of its charmed power. The splendor and magnificence of hotel life have fairly reached their zenith here, and no one can hope to see "modern improvements" carried further, unless we can be supplied with patent appliances for mastication, and thus save that wear and tear upon our incisors and molars, which now result in no small advantage to the dentists. Those who have suffered, as I have, the miserable accommodations of "prairie hotels," where all things are not only held in common, but *very common* at that, know how to appreciate the luxury of a home where inconvenience is unknown, and where the mind is constantly gratified by that succession of novelty and pleasure which adds zest to the spirit, and animates even the physical powers.

Not the least of the accommodations to us lady guests are the capital facilities afforded us in the immediate vicinity, indeed, in the very hotel, for the supplying of all our little necessary articles of wardrobe. Here Genin, the Napoleon of costumers, holds forth his varied bazaar of a thousand wonders to tempt the fancy and beguile the unwilling dollars from the pocket. What an establishment! or, as a Westerner would say, "What a smart bit of a place!" No less than twelve distinct departments, where every thing essential for a complete and fashionable outfit can be obtained. How many a dusty, dirty Californian, in blue jean and red flannel, has here been so suddenly transformed into a being of beauty and fashion that he scarcely knew himself when he paid his first attentions to the mirror! And to the ladies, what a place of interest! The furs of Russian sable and royal ermine, lace of elegant workmanship, the fancy articles, delicate work-boxes, with caskets of jewels, etc., etc.,—the mind actually wearies in looking over the magnificent assortment; but I am consuming, I fear, too much of your valuable space in these exciting election times. Still, I must dilate upon scenes new to me, something that is not connected with the jingling of cars, the clatter of rickety engines, and the dirt and dust of western travel. Adieu! when you hear from me again it may be perchance upon some western plain, where the joyous sounds of the St. Nicholas are never heard, where primeval stillness reigns supreme, and where the luxuries of a dining room, resplendent with brilliant luster and a thousand appetizing viands, are never seen; indeed, where Nature is reduced to the solid realities of pork and hominy, or mayhap I shall drop you a line from Chicago, the Empire City of the West.

XXIX.

Growth of Chicago.—Commerce.—Fashions, &c.—Nomination of Honorable R. S. Malony for Congress.—Speeches of Colonel Richardson and Colonel Carpenter.—The Fifth Avenue of Chicago.

TREMONT HOUSE, CHICAGO, September 21, 1856.

I AM more and more surprised every day I pass in Chicago at its gigantic enterprise and wonderful improvements. It is but twenty years since it was incorporated as a city; now it has a population of a hundred thousand, and ornamented with fine substantial buildings, enjoys all the luxuries and conveniences of living. I am told that the last year's exports of grain alone were over twenty millions. Vessels are sent out direct to England. On the 17th. instant a new and splendid schooner, the "Dean Richmond," left her dock for Liverpool. She had on board four thousand seven hundred bushels of grain, and stopped at Milwaukie to complete her cargo.

In railroads, manufactures and all internal improvements, Chicago is at least a quarter of a century in advance of her sister cities. In gayety and fashion she is entitled to rank A number one. Her wealth and luxury of living are proverbial, whilst her belles and beaux seem the impersonation of nature's noblemen and women. No city in the West can boast of more sumptuous and luxurious accommodations for strangers. She maintains several large, well-regulated, first-class hotels, one of which, the Tremont, situated on the corner of Lake and Dearborn streets, is magnificently and tastefully furnished, and without regard to expense. The conveniences and comforts of the establishment have already secured and must, in time to come, insure it a large share of public patronage. The first thought and desire of a weary traveler, on reaching a strange place, is to find a well-kept hotel—one where his every comfort is cared for, and every thing conspires to make him feel home-like and contented. The Tremont is such a one.

The "Ladies' Ordinary" is very handsomely finished and fitted up; tables profusely furnished with all the appetizing luxuries of the season, and served in perfect order and elegance. The *cuisine* is the very best; and well-drilled waiters are constantly on the look-out to find out the requirements of the guests. Dinner from one to three o'clock. Guests can walk into this quiet, elegant and well-appointed dining-room, seat themselves at one of those tempting tables, order whatever they choose from the *carte de diner*, and discuss it quietly, and at their own time and leisure. This is choosing one's own time and convenience for taking meals and refreshments, instead of suiting it to others; and thus avoiding all the uncomfortable crushing and scrambling of a single *table d'hôte.*

Those who visit Chicago should go to this magnificent establishment, and place themselves under the care of those gentlemanly men, the Messrs. Gage, Brother and Drake, the proprietors and conductors of this excellent house, who take great pains to render the stay of their guests in every way pleasant; and with the splendid location of the house itself, the careful attention of its proprietors, and the high character it enjoys as a first-class hotel ,perfect in all its appointments, it is just the place to pass time in Chicago pleasantly.

The Democracy of the first congressional district held their convention to nominate a candidate for Congress, at Freeport, Stephenson county, Illinois, July 7th, and unanimously agreed upon the Honorable R. S. Malony, who formerly represented his district with so much honor to himself and usefulness to his constituents. A mass meeting was then held in the public square where Colonel William A. Richardson, the democratic nominee for governor, addressed the immense crowd of people for nearly two hours, in a speech replete with wit, argument and eloquence. He reviewed the history of the slavery agitation—defended the principles of the Kansas-Nebraska Act; and, not content with defense, he carried the war into Africa (by the way, this classical expression has a peculiar significance when applied to attack upon the Black Republican army), and showed that Colonel Bissel (the Fremont candidate for governor), had voted for the same principle in the Utah, and New Mexico, and Washington Bills, and spoke in favor of them, including Mormondom. Colonel R. built a wall of fire around his opponent, from which, in November, there will be no escape, except upon that retired and quiet stream, Salt river.

After he concluded, Colonel R. B. Carpenter,

of Chicago, addressed the audience for an hour and a half. In analyzing political character, and describing the various shades of political part es, he possesses great strength and originality of style and expression, with a precision of logical reasoning, interspersed with wit, anecdote and flowers of rhetoric, which made a marked impression upon the large audience present. Colonel C. a year since removed from the State of Kentucky to this city, and will, doubtless, become one of the master spirits of the Democracy of the whole State of Illinois. Young, gallant, chivalrous, learned and eloquent, he will wear fitly the mantle of greatness, as he wields aptly the scepter of eloquence. I may add to this, that he is already a great favorite with the Democratic party, and thoroughly national and orthodox in his political tenets.

You can set it down as a fixed fact, that the Democracy will sweep this State at the fall election by an old-fashioned majority.

Michigan avenue is to Chicago what Fifth avenue is to New York, the favorite street for private dwellings. On the east side it runs directly on the lake shore. It is a mile and a half in length, and has an elevation of twelve or fourteen feet above

the water. The houses are built only on the west side, leaving the view of the lake entirely unobstructed. There are many fine private residences on this street, both in size and style, which may be fairly ranked as palaces. It is one of the most pleasant and most interesting walks in the Union, having a pure cool breeze, a full view of the lake, which, as far as the eye can reach, is dotted over with vessels and sailing craft of all kinds. From this promenade may be seen constantly passing and repassing trains of twenty or thirty cars on the railroad track, built on the lake, the inside line being four hundred feet from the east side of the avenue, and in sight the finest, most substantial, and largest dépôt in the world. On the north side, which, toward the lake shore, is rather more quiet and retired, are many fine cottages of the best suburban styles, adorned with conservatories and gardens, and embowered in groves of locust, ash and oak.

At present the city is remarkably healthy, and weather cool and delightful.

XXX.

Illinois Politics.—Mr. Douglas.—Mr. Lincoln.—Colonel Carpenter.—The Result of the Present Contest.

CHICAGO, ILL., August 1, 1858.

A SINGULAR political condition was that of Illinois in 1856, Mr. Buchanan receiving ten thousand votes more than Fremont, while Colonel Bissell beat Colonel Richardson, the regular Democratic nominee, over eight thousand, and this while the latter received two thousand more votes than Buchanan. The Know Nothings had a candidate for governor, Judge Morris, but he was not able to command the party strength, falling behind Mr. Fillmore about twenty thousand votes.

The only question that has changed the aspect of affairs since is the question of the admission of Kansas under the Lecompton constitution.

The opposition of Senator Douglas to that measure, and the reasons assigned by him, are too well known to require a repetition. That the effect of the schism will be injurious to the party, none can doubt; but that it will be detrimental to the senator, so far as his return to the Senate is concerned, I do not believe. He, in this respect, has played his game well. The Republican papers, orators, and members of Congress, have not only coincided in his views, but have actively supported him in his course upon this question. And that in his case is the issue to be decided on in November. *They* told their rank and file that the senator was right, until enough of them believed it to return him to the Senate. They have called "spirits from the vasty deep." Mr. Douglas may, and probably will, lose some Democratic districts, but he will gain in some Republican districts more than enough to counterbalance his losses. This will be accomplished in part by running Republicans and Know Nothings friendly to Douglas in close districts, and thus distracting the opposition by using their own men.

But there is another reason that leads me to this conclusion. It is this. The general sentiment of the North is one of opposition to slavery, and especially to the admission of more slave States. There is no principle involved in the submission or non-submission of a State constitution to the people, whether we take as our guide the theory or practice of the government. But the people of the North know that a majority of the citizens of Kansas are for a free State; and hence, if Mr. Douglas's programme is carried out, and the constitution submitted to them, that slavery can not find place among her institutions. And this is the real principle that will, in my opinion, triumphantly return Mr. Douglas to the Senate. Three parties have already held monster meetings here. The first, in point of time and numbers, was on the return of Mr. Douglas, when he was received in a manner highly complimentary, and doubtless very gratifying to him. He made a speech to the assembled thousands from the balcony of the Tremont House. The speech has been published and read throughout the country, and I will not extend this communication by adverting to its topics. The senator has too long been a prominent actor on the public stage, his splendid ability too well known and generally recognized, to require from me comment. In manner, he combines force and *grace*. His head is noble, almost Websterian. His voice not unpleasant, and altogether he is a most effective popular speaker.

The next, following the same order as before, was the great Republican gathering, which was addressed by Mr. Lincoln, the Republican candidate for the Senate. The meeting was large and enthusiastic. Mr. Lincoln is not much known out of Illinois. In person, he is tall and awkward; in manner, ungainly. His face is certainly ugly, but not repulsive; on the contrary, the good humor, generosity and intellect beaming from it, makes the eye love to linger there until you almost fancy him good-looking. He is a man of decided talents. On the stump, ready, humorous, argumentative, and tells an anecdote with inconceivable quaintness and effect. He is honest as a man, and enthusiastic as a politician. He is an able lawyer, and that is the true field of his fame; for, unless I am mistaken in my estimate above, he will for some years, at least, remain an ornament to that noble profession.

Last, and least in point of numbers and enthusiasm, the administration Democracy held a meeting in Metropolitan Hall. The spacious edifice was crammed full, though it was easy to see and hear that the multitude did not sympathize with the orators. Colonel Carpenter opened the ball. He is a young man, who removed from Kentucky to this city in 1855, and canvassed a large portion of the State for the Democratic ticket in 1856. In person, he is tall, with a good figure, a fine voice, and eyes that are absolutely sleepy (it would be more poetical to say dreamy, but sleepy is the word). There is nothing in his face or appearance to indicate the man, unless it be some lines plowed, not by years, but thought, and an habitual shade of sadness that rests always upon his face when in repose. When addressing a popular audience, in moments of enthusiasm, his eyes brighten to a blaze, and his features do the bidding of his mind with wonderful facility. *Sarcasm*, *scorn*, *contempt*, are mirrored with faithful accuracy, while, in his loftier bursts of eloquence, he seems the embodiment of the devoted, unselfish patriot. His thoughts are bold and clear, his diction smooth and flowing, or terse and anti-musical, as suits his purpose and the occasion. He does not attempt to win a forensic battle by stratagetic movements, but marshals his thoughts in solid phalanx, and drops upon the enemy and takes the position at the point of the bayonet. He utters the boldest and most unpopular propositions, in a manner and with a voice which seems to say, Sir, *listen* to me, and you *shall* be convinced. He has a fertile imagination, a soaring fancy, and deep pathos, and yet keeps them all in such subjection to his judgment that he is eminently a practical speaker. It is true there are flowers on either hand, but there is also a well-defined path along which the orator has passed. From his few published speeches the reader can determine the correctness of these remarks. The speech on the occasion referred to was equally denunciatory of Douglasism and Republicanism. It has had a wide circulation, and speaks for itself. Mr. Fitch, the District Attorney, and others, addressed the meeting, but I have neither time nor space to follow them.

XXXI.

A Trip to the White Mountains.—The Flume House.

FLUME HOUSE, WHITE MOUNTAINS, N. H., August 6, 1858.

AFTER having had a good, warm supper, and hovered over a rousing wood fire for half an hour, I think I am sufficiently thawed out to give an account of myself. It is sufficient to say that I was smitten with the White Mountain fever on Monday last, and taking my old and favorite line, when going East, the Norwich and Worcester, I soon found myself *en route* for the White Mountains of New Hampshire. As it may be interesting to others to know the route to take, I will put down the items. First, the Norwich and Worcester line of steamers. You arrive in Worcester the morning after leaving New York in time for the six o'clock train for Nashua, Concord and Wells River. It is better to leave the train at Plymouth, and take the stage, twenty-three miles to the Flume House, which is located just at the entrance of the Franconia Notch.

I found the stage ride the most pleasant and delightful of any part of the journey. The road is not what most people might expect to find. It follows the valley of the Pemigewasset River the whole distance, which grows gradually more and more narrow. The scenery is so variegated with gently-sloping acclivities, steep and rugged precipices and the projecting cliffs of the mountains on either side, that the eye is never wearied of the scenery. The Pemigewasset seems like an angry torrent, rushing in wild majesty over ragged stones and through narrow gorges, and then gliding out quietly and smoothly as the surface of a lake.

We had two stage loads of passengers from Plymouth, where we arrived at one o'clock and took dinner. We reached the Flume House, my present quarters, a little before six. The tops of the mountains, almost ever since we entered the Pemigewasset valley, have been covered with mists and fogs. The weather, too, has been gradually growing colder, rendering overcoats, in riding, indispensable, and fires in the hotel exceedingly agreeable. A bright wood fire now blazes up before me as I write, the first time I ever recollect of needing artificial caloric in August to keep the body warm. To-morrow

I shall explore the sights in the vicinity, of which I hear there are several of interest. The Profile Mountain is just visible to the north of us, its bare and rugged sides looming up twelve hundred feet almost perpendicularly above the road at its base. Mount Lafayette is also in sight, but its top has been enveloped in a dense fog all the afternoon. The Flume is about a mile from the hotel. Echo Lake is also hard by, with other points of interest.

It is a matter of wonder that more people do not visit these mountains. Just twenty-four hours of easy travel from New York has set me down here in the very midst of gigantic mountains and splendid scenery, where one may feast his eyes and revel in imagination to his heart's content. Such a phenomenon as a warm night, I am told, has not been known here this summer. People who come here sleep as soundly as in winter, and rise refreshed and strengthened. The general impression among people is, I think, that it is difficult to reach the White Mountains, that the roads are rough and the hotels poor, but such is not the case. The roads are smooth, the hotels large and commodious, and every attention is paid to the wants of guests.

New Hampshire is a much more pleasant and

inviting State than I expected to find it. Nearly all the land seems well cultivated, and tolerably productive. But I am astonished to find crops so backward. Rye is not yet harvested. Some fields are green, and will not be ready for the reaper in some time. Corn and New Hampshire, I take it, are no friends. All I have seen to-day looks sickly and feeble, and will hardly pay for the gathering. Indeed, I have seen corn in southern Illinois in June larger than some fields I have seen to-day in "top-gallant." There is an air of neatness and thriftiness about the farm houses which is very agreeable. The only wonder is, that with so little arable land the people should evidently get so good a livelihood. I do n't know what they sell. It certainly is not grain.

XXXII.

The Flume. — The Cascades. — The Old Man of the Mountains.

PROFILE HOUSE, N. H., August 7, 1858.

THIS has been almost a *dies non*, so far as seeing the mountains is concerned. The rain has either poured down in torrents or kept drizzling in a dull, heavy mist from the clouds, which almost seem to touch our heads. This spot is not the White Mountains proper, but the Franconia, a range scarcely less interesting. In the rear of the Flume House a mountain of the same name towers up, a view from the summit of which, it is said, gives a splendid view of the entire valley. As for views, I am compelled to take them all upon hearsay, for *I* can't see any thing but mists and fogs.

I have one exception, however, to this remark. Before I left the Flume House, which is only five miles from the Profile, I visited the Flume itself. It consists of a narrow gorge, through which flows a rolling, tumbling stream, coming down from the heights above in the wildest confusion. Instead of precipitating the stream over the perpendicular edge of the cliff, nature has cut for it the gorge referred to in the rocks. Below the Flume are the Cascades, where the stream, for a distance of some six hundred feet, falls over the surface of a smooth rock, up whose slippery sides the traveler is forced to wend his way in order to reach the natural curiosity above. The spot is well worth seeing, and surpasses in wildness and strange singularity any thing I have ever seen. In our party were a lady and gentleman who had traveled over all Europe, and they asserted they had never seen any thing so strikingly picturesque. The sides of the gorge rise abruptly some sixty or seventy feet, while the stream struggles through it with a low, gurgling sound. Queerest of all, nature in one of her most fantastic freaks has detached a huge rock, weighing several tons, from the side of the mountain and rolled it into the gorge, where it has lodged in the most narrow part of the chasm, some thirty or forty feet above the waters. The greatest wonder is what holds it there, for it hangs in such a peculiar position that it would seem to take but a jar or a jolt to send it tumbling into the stream below. A path of planks has been constructed up through the Flume from rock to rock until you can walk directly under the overhanging rock itself. Some will not venture there, arguing that as the rock is sure to fall *some* time, it is just as likely to come down when they are under it as at any other period. Our party did not take counsel of this cautious argument, but clambered their way over the trembling planks, unterrified by the torrent below. The view immediately under the rock is somewhat "pokerish," to use a common but expressive quotation. We soon, however, hurried back to the hotel, glad to get by a warm fire and out of the incessant "drizzle, drizzle," which seemed to dampen us completely through.

We did not visit the Pool, another curiosity near the Flume House, on account of the rain, but hurried on to this place, the Profile House. Most of the way it rained as usual. Indeed, we seem to be living in the clouds where the rain is manufactured for the regions below. This house is 500 feet higher up the mountain than the Flume. It is exactly in the Notch of the Franconia Mountains, and is considered the coldest place in New Hampshire, except, perhaps, the top of Mount Washington. The wind draws through the narrow gorge of the mountains, which here almost approach each other. On our left to-day coming up was Profile Mountain, near the summit of which is the peak called "The Old Man of the Mountain." This consists of the exact profile of a man's face. I did not expect to-day to get a glimpse of it, but as we came up, "the Old Man" had the politeness to take off his cap of mist and cloud and allow us to inspect his phiz. Our driver says it is eighty feet from the Old Man's chin to his forehead. If such be the fact, he may be said to be a long-faced old fellow. At all events, he looks sufficiently solemn. Besides, he seems care-worn. I could detect deep fissures and wrinkles in his sides, which are as barren as the Russ pavement in Broadway, and about as slippery. After you get further around the mountain towards the Profile House, the sides are covered with trees and verdure, but in front the Old Man has evidently seen hard times. He has been looking down the Pemigewasset valley, I expect, ever since the world began. At any rate, I will give anybody liberty to contradict who *knows* to the contrary. The Profile Lake or "Old Man's Mirror," as some poetical tourists call it, is just at the base of the mountain. It is a beautiful sheet of water, and clear as crystal.

Opposite the Old Man of the Mountain is Mount Lafayette, which is only five hundred feet lower than Mount Washington. But I could not see it. It was vailed in black, heavy clouds, which most of the time were pouring down their contents in much greater quantities than were agreeable.

The Profile House is delightfully situated, and seems to be a place of great resort. We found it almost full. There can not be less than two hundred people here to-night. It is only eleven miles from the railroad at Littleton, but I think the route I came decidedly the best. You have the beautiful stage ride, see the Flume, and get here almost as soon as by the railroad.

To-night it rains as if it had never rained before, and I am in hopes it will clear up and give us a fair day to-morrow. The weather here is several degrees colder than at the Flume House. The doors of the hotel are all closed, and there are large wood fires in the parlors. Wood is cheap and plenty. The vast acres of forest in the vicinity belong to no one, and each man helps himself. Timber is plenty, but the men are scarce. There is not a single dwelling, except one Indian hut, between here and the Flume. The town of Lincoln, in which the Flume House is situated, has but eleven voters, all told! What a glorious place it must be! Every man can have an office!

Yesterday a large bear was caught near here. They say it was amazingly poor, and looked as if it had seen the hardest kind of times. I saw one of its fore feet, which was a solid specimen of a paw, and one which I would much prefer not to encounter. If these are the "natives" of this region, I desire not to make their acquaintance.

XXXIII.

Montreal.—The Victoria Tubular Bridge.

DONEGANA HOTEL, MONTREAL, August 10, 1858.

LEFT the White Mountains on Friday with the 11 o'clock train, and arrived in Montreal the same evening. It rained during almost the entire day; in fact this is the first clear weather I have seen since leaving home. The road from Gorham to this place lies through the upper portions of New Hampshire, Vermont and Lower Canada. It crosses the head waters of the Connecticut river, and for many miles runs through vast pine forests, which do not seem as yet to have been scarcely touched by the woodman's ax. Wild and uncultivated, the scenery is all that the lover of primeval solitude can ask. When the cars reached Island Pond, in Vermont, a beautiful sheet of water, clasping in its crystal embrace three or four beautiful islands, Uncle Samuel's custom house officers examined our baggage. The examination is not very rigid, consisting in simply inquiring what the trunks, &c., contained. When assured that they held nothing but ordinary traveling apparel, the indefatigable officer solemnly crossed them with "a piece of chalk," and his duty had been performed.

At this place, too, the cars halt for dinner. The Grand Trunk Railway have here a very commodious dépôt, in fact all the stations on their road are supplied with very substantial houses for passengers. Soon after leaving Island Pond, we cross the Boundary Line, and are in the dominions of Queen Victoria. The country still looks bleak and cold. The pine forests begin to show occasionally the inroads of the intrepid pioneer, but generally they are dark, drear, and seemingly impenetrable. The road here strikes the head waters of the Coaticook river, a small stream which finally empties into the St. Francis river, a very considerable body of water. The route down this valley is exceedingly agreeable. Sometimes, as the cars strike a summit, you can see for miles, the eye taking in nothing but long unbroken tracts of pines. Again, evidences of settlement are seen, until, as you reach the St. Francis river, the country becomes well settled and apparently carefully cultivated.

Vast masses of lumber are rafted down the St. Francis, forming one of the most important features in the business of this section.

As we approach Montreal, the country becomes as level as the prairies of the West, and the land exhibits a high state of cultivation. Far as the eye can reach is one expanse of country, dotted with farm houses and waving with crops almost ready for harvesting. Wheat here is still quite green, not much of it yet having assumed a ripe appearance. The crops, both of this grain and oats, seem very good. I notice, however, an immense quantity of what are called in New York State "Canada thistles." From St. Hilaire to Montreal the fields are literally covered with them, and how the farmers manage to gather their crops or work with any degree of comfort among such a mass of prickly nuisances I can not imagine.

To-day I have been examining Montreal. The city has a queer, quaint appearance. The people are evidently not as progressive as with us. The business part of the town looks somewhat modern, but in other portions it retains the old French style of the early settlement. The houses are substantially built, close to the sidewalks, which are very narrow. Notre Dame and Great St. James are the principal streets. Notre Dame somewhat resembles Washington street, of Boston, though it is not so lively or busy. In fact, Montreal is a dull place, and needs, I apprehend, a little more infusion of American energy to wake it up. An enterprising Yankee here might make a fortune by establishing a line of omnibuses. It is said the attempt was made a few years since, but the drivers of the cabs, *calaches* and other uncivilized looking vehicles they have here, burnt up his stables and horses, and the poor man was compelled to fly the town. This summer another Yankee has undertaken a baggage and passenger express from the cars, coming on board the train before it stops, getting the checks, &c., as is customary on the roads to New York, but he is threatened with death if he do n't quit this innovation upon ancient customs. Our driver assured us to-day, when taking a ride to the mountain, that "he would catch it before the summer was over."

The Victoria Tubular Bridge, in connection with the Grand Trunk Railway, will form, when completed, the most important public work of Canada. This line of railway is intended to form a direct line of communication through the entire

Canadian provinces, from west to east, ending at the capacious harbor of Portland, in Maine, as its eastern terminus. The road is constructed throughout in the most substantial manner, and excepting the road from Norwich to Worcester, in Massachusetts, I never rode on its superior. It is famous for its strong and massive bridges, the most important one of which already completed is the Saint Anns, over the Ottawa river. But the bridges already built, and, in fact, the bridges of the world, pale in insignificance before the gigantic Victoria Tubular Bridge now in course of construction at this place. It crosses the Saint Lawrence about a mile and a half above the central part of the town, and at a place where the water is so rapid the boats can not go up the current. When the rapidity of the stream is taken into consideration, and the fact that a coffer-dam has to be made for each pier, the water pumped out, and excavations made below the bed of the river, in some cases as far as thirteen feet, before a suitable foundation for the pier can be found, some idea of the immense labor of the undertaking can be formed. Then let it be remembered that there are to be twenty-four of these massive cut stone piers to sustain the twenty-five iron arches; and that these iron arches are made of heavy wrought iron plates, from a quarter to half an inch in thickness, fastened together with innumerable rivets, and that these arches extend a distance of one mile and three quarters! When the mind fairly comprehends these facts, it will begin to understand the gigantic character of this work.

All will recollect what an excitement was occasioned in England by the completion of the Britannia Tubular Bridge across the Menai Straits; but this work is an insignificant one, in point of size, compared with the Victoria Bridge. The Britannia Bridge is only fifteen hundred and thirteen feet long, though its longest tube is four hundred and sixty feet. The Victoria Bridge, as I have stated, will be one mile and three quarters, the longest tube being three hundred and thirty feet. Our visit to this wonderful work was greatly enhanced in interest by Mr. J. W. Woodford, the superintending engineer, who has special charge of putting up the tubes, and who explained to us all the details of the manner of construction. Mr. Stephenson, the renowned inventor of the bridge, is not in this country, Mr. James Hodges having the general direction of the work. From Mr. Woodford we learn that the contractors, Messrs. Jackson, Peto, Brassy and Betts, have now about three hundred men employed. They are prosecuting the work with all the expedition possible, but the advance is necessarily slow. The ice in the Saint Lawrence does not get out before May, and the cold weather sets in by the first of November, so that it leaves only about six months in the year for work. Four years have already been consumed, and it is estimated it will take at least two more to complete it, should they have good luck. This year they have had a good deal of difficulty with the dams, one having broken away three times. Fourteen piers are now completed, and it is hoped to have eight more done this year. Three tubes are finished, and it is expected that five more will be put up before the season closes.

The tubes are well worth a study. The iron is imported from England, already manufactured. They are made in Birkenhead, opposite Liverpool. Nothing is made here but the rivets, for which the contractors have a machine on purpose. The sheets of iron are about twelve feet in length and two and a half in width (I have not the exact figures). These are riveted to T and L iron. The tubes nearest the shore are nineteen feet high and seventeen feet wide, and increase in size as the span increases in length. The center tube, over the three hundred and thirty feet span, is twenty-two feet high and seventeen feet wide. Each span contains about two hundred and forty tons of iron, and each span is from two hundred and forty eight to three hundred and thirty feet in length.

It is calculated that the buttress of each pier will have to bear the pressure of seventy thousand tons of ice when the winter breaks up, and the ice comes sweeping down the Saint Lawrence. Mr. Woodford informed us that last spring it was piled in some places thirty feet above the bridge. The highest span of the bridge is sixty feet from the water. It seems like being in Pandemonium to enter the tubes at present, where they are at work. It is perfectly dark, except what little light may be dimly discovered at the entrance, the few streaks that pour through the yet unriveted holes, and the light of the smiths' fires, used in heating the rivets. Add to the smoke thus occasioned the incessant thumping of perhaps some hundred and fifty hammers, and a faint idea of the scene is obtained. Where Vulcan forged his thunderbolts could not have been a place of such deafening noise. Perhaps old John Ford, in describing Tophet, had no intention of picturing the building of an iron tubular bridge, and yet he did it most accurately:

> "A black and hollow vault
> Where day is never seen; there shines no sun,
> But flaming horrors of consuming fire;
> A lightless sulphur cloak'd with smoky fogs
> Of an infected darkness."

When this tubular bridge is completed, it will most assuredly be the greatest work of the kind on this continent, and, in fact, in the world. Its cost will be about $7,500,000, and it will attract thousands of visitors to Montreal; for it will be in mechanical skill and workmanship what Niagara is in nature. The Canadians certainly deserve great praise for their enterprise and activity, and it is no wonder they are proud of this stupendous work.

XXXIV.

Trip from Chicago.—Railroads.—Pennsylvania Central.—The Alleghanies.—Scenery.—The St. Nicholas Hotel.

ST. NICHOLAS HOTEL, NEW YORK, July 14, 1859.

ON the 8th instant, I left the "Garden City," at seven o'clock, A. M., on the Pittsburg, Fort Wayne and Chicago Railroad, and was rolled away at a rapid rate through a pleasant and fertile country in Illinois, Indiana and Ohio, where the crops seemed abundant, and where I was told the wheat already harvested is of superior quality. We passed through may thriving towns along the line of the road that are rapidly advancing in material prosperity and external beauty. The result of the modern system of pressing events into a narrow compass is, that life seems a succession of pleasant changes, and what used to cost a week's travel is now accomplished with pleasant ease in a single day; so that we live now-a-days as much, if not so long, as in the camel-riding days of the olden time.

The whole road over which I traveled is in good order, the cars in excellent condition, and the officials, from Colonel Boss, the gentlemanly general agent for the West, and the conductors, down to the brakemen, are courteous, polite and attentive to the wants of the traveling public. The refreshments, no small item in traveling, are first rate at Fort Wayne, Cresline and Alliance. It is a safe, speedy route, and meets, in the increased receipts, a well-merited reward.

On the 9th instant I left Pittsburg, which is noted for its great manufacturing and mineral products, the former consisting chiefly of iron in every form. Glass and glassware are also extensively manufactured, and the surrounding country abounds in mineral wealth. Traffic in coal is extensive, amounting to many millions of bushels per annum.

I noticed, in taking our departure from the city, the extensive engine-houses, machine-shops, warehouses, &c., of the Pennsylvania Railroad Company, situated in the suburbs of the busy city. The engine-house is said to be one thousand feet in circumference, affording accommodation for forty-six locomotives, which is believed to be the largest house of the kind in America. Five miles east of

Pittsburg we pass through East Liberty, where the city merchant retires from the turmoil of business, and the smoke of the iron city, to obtain for himself and family social enjoyment and relaxation from business. The whole country is dotted with splendid country houses.

Ten miles east of Pittsburg we pass through the battle ground where General Braddock met with his miserable defeat. Two miles further we enter the region abounding in bituminous coal, known as the Pittsburg Gas Seam, much of which is shipped to the eastern cities, New York, Philadelphia, &c., to be used in providing the ever-useful gas light. Mines are opened at many points, and give evidence of great activity in that branch of trade. I was informed that the railroad company ship eastward fifty thousand tons per annum. Forty miles east of Pittsburg we passed through the Loyal Hanna valley, a beautiful, fertile country, in the midst of which the thriving village of Latrobe is situated. This valley is the grand climax to all Alleghany aspirations. Let the whole world come and look at it, and be silent, for it is a temple worthy of the Eternal!

After leaving Blairville Intersection we passed

through the gap in Chestnut Ridge, the road being located above the Conemaugh river about a hundred and sixty feet. As we glided along, the outlines of the many peaks were very distinct; not a cloud to obstruct a single feature of their colossal proportions; and while they had already taken the shadow of evening upon their brows, it still reflected back the last rays of the sinking sun. I sat by the window and watched the last golden beam as it crept to the utmost peak, and thence seemed to glide into heaven! The sight was beautiful: it resembled love—love that lingers longest when you are above and beyond its mockeries.

Eighty-one miles from Pittsburg we reach Johnstown, at the foot of the Alleghanies, where we find the extensive iron rail mills and furnaces of the Cambria Iron Company. The product of this vast establishment is said to exceed one hundred tons of rails per day, giving employment to over three thousand men. The rails are principally used on western and southern roads, accessible by rail or the Ohio river. Leaving Johnstown, we begin ascending the mountain. Twenty-two miles from the base we reach the Cresson Hotel, quite a popular summer resort. The hotels are extensive, and well managed by Mr. Campbell, proprietor of the Saint Lawrence Hotel, Philadelphia. A few miles east of Cresson we pass throught the great Alleghany mountain tunnel, three thousand seven hundred feet in length, which is a magnificent work, being substantially arched and in perfect condition.

Emerging from the tunnel, we have before us the grandest and most beautiful mountain scenery which it has ever been our good fortune to look upon. The blending of mountain peaks with the fertile valleys far below, presents a picture that all lovers of nature must greatly admire.

The road is one of the most permanent in the world, having been constructed at great expense. The iron is heavy, and of the most approved patterns. Cross-ties larger than we have seen in any road, all laid in broken stone, which render the roadway firm, furnishes excellent drainage, and, at the same time, is a perfect preventive against the clouds of dust, a source of great annoyance on many roads in America. All things considered, we regard the Pennsylvania Central as the railroad *par excellence* of the country. A ride over it is a great treat to the lover of fine scenery, or the traveler who consults comfort.

In four hours and thirty-five minutes after leaving Pittsburg we arrived at the Logan House, Altoona, and were surprised to find a first-class hotel, capable of accommodating over two hundred guests. It is a rare treat for the weary traveler to meet with such a house. We concluded to rest here for the night, and resume our going east in the morning. We witnessed the operation of a very valuable railroad improvement known as Longbridge's Graduating Car Brake, which has been adopted by the Pennsylvania Railroad Company. This invention gives to the engineer entire control of all the brakes in the train, and enables him to stop in one half the distance that can now be done with the old mode of applying the brakes by hand. It gives a very perceptible quietness to the movement of trains, as brakemen are not constantly called by the whistle to apply the brakes. This improvement is essential to the safety of human life, and should be at once adopted by all railroad companies.

From Altoona to Harrisburg the scenery is less grand, but very picturesque. The railroad follows the coy windings of the river Juniata, of whose beauty the poet has sung. It is wildly natural and graceful, shut in by a labyrinth of mountains. This end of the road is in excellent order, the conductors polite and attentive, and the best hotels in the country. It is a wonder that this trip over the Alleghanies is not the most favorite of the excursions. We are indebted for much of our information concerning the road to the gentlemanly superintendent, Thomas A. Scott, Esquire. From Harrisburg to Philadelphia the road passes through the finest agricultural region in America, but want of space must defer a full description.

A few words about my old home, the Saint Nicholas, and I will close this rambling letter. It is three years since I gazed upon its ample parlors and its brilliant dining-rooms; but three years do not seem to have faded its beauties or dimmed its brilliancy. The same dazzling glow of gold and crimson strikes the eye; the carpets are just as soft, and the chandeliers shed down the same mellow and undulating light. The crowd still throngs its palatial passage-ways, and as eagerly as ever crowd its drawing-rooms. Broadway, with its ceaseless thunder of vehicles, roars as loudly as ever; the sidewalks seem even more crowded, and every thing reminds me, an old New Yorker, that

I am again in the vortex of that cosmopolitan city, which is an epitome of every nation and tongue under the sun. And the Saint Nicholas is an epitome of New York. No other hotel so truly represents the ever-varying features of New York life. Here the gallant and chivalric southerner may be seen, full of the proud dignity of his clime; and not far off, the calculating Yankee, shrewdly cogitating upon stocks or merchandise. Over all, however, this palatial caravansery spreads its wings like a bird of beautiful plumage, shielding all from storm and rain, and feeding the inner man with those luxuries which make the heart glad. There is only one New York, and only one Saint Nicholas. Ease, comfort, luxury, and home are combined with oriental magnificence; and it is no wonder that thousands annually throng its halls and corridors, and partake of its generous hospitality.

CATALOGUE

OF THE

PUBLICATIONS

OF

RUDD & CARLETON,

130 Grand Street,

(BROOKS BUILDING, COR. OF BROADWAY,)

New York.

VERNON GROVE;

By Mrs. CAROLINE H. GLOVER. "A Novel which will give its author high rank among the novelists of the day."—*Atlantic Monthly.* 12mo., Muslin, price $1 00

BALLAD OF BABIE BELL,

And other Poems. By THOMAS BAILEY ALDRICH. The first selected collection of verses by this author. 12mo Exquisitely printed, and bound in muslin, price 75 cents.

TRUE LOVE NEVER DID RUN SMOOTH.

An Eastern Tale, in Verse. By THOMAS BAILEY ALDRICH, author of "Babie Bell, and other Poems." Printed on colored plate paper. Muslin, price 50 cents

BEATRICE CENCI.

A Historical Novel. By F. D. GUERRAZZI. Translated from the original Italian by LUIGI MONTI. Muslin, two volumes in one, with steel portrait price $1 25.

ISABELLA ORSINI.

A new historical novel. By F. D. GUERRAZZI, author of "Beatrice Cenci." Translated by MONTI, of Harvard College. With steel portrait. Muslin, price $1 25.

DOCTOR ANTONIO.

A charming Love Tale of Italy. By G. RUFFINI, author of "Lorenzo Benoni," "Dear Experience," &c From the last London edition. Muslin, price $1 00.

DEAR EXPERIENCE.

A Tale. By G. RUFFINI, author of "Doctor Antonio," "Lorenzo Benoni," &c. With illustrations by Leech, *of the London Punch.* 12mo. Muslin, price $1 00.

A BACHELOR'S STORY.

By Oliver Bunce. Upon the thread of a pleasant story the author has strung a wampum of love, philosophy and humor. 12mo. Muslin, price $1 00.

LIFE OF HUGH MILLER,

Author of "Schools and Schoolmasters," "Old Red Sandstone," &c. From the last Glasgow edition. Prepared by Thomas N. Brown. Muslin, price $1 00

AFTERNOON OF UNMARRIED LIFE.

An interesting theme, admirably treated, and combined with strong common sense. Companion to "Woman's Thoughts." From London edition. Price $1 00

LECTURES OF LOLA MONTEZ,

Including her "Autobiography," "Wits and Women of Paris," "Comic Aspect of Love," "Beautiful Women," "Gallantry," &c. Muslin, steel portrait, price $1 00.

K. N. PEPPER PAPERS.

Containing the Writings and laughable Verses of one of the first humorous contributors to "*Knickerbocker Magazine.*" With Illustrations. Muslin, price $1 00.

CURIOSITIES OF NATURAL HISTORY.

By Francis T. Buckland, M.A. A sparkling collection of surprises in Natural History, and the charm of a lively narrative. From 4th London edition, price $1 25.

BROWN'S CARPENTER'S ASSISTANT.

The best practical work on Architecture; with Plans for every description of Building. Illustrated with over 200 Plates. Strongly bound in leather, price $5 00.

THE VAGABOND.

A volume of Miscellaneous Papers, treating in colloquia sketches upon Literature, Society, and Art. By ADAM BADEAU. Bound in muslin, 12mo, price $1 00.

COSMOGONY;

Or, the Mysteries of Creation. A remarkable book, being an Analysis of the First Chapter of Genesis. By THOMAS A. DAVIES. Octavo, muslin, price $2 00

FOLLOWING THE DRUM;

Or, Glimpses of Frontier Life. Being brilliant Sketches of Recruiting Incidents on the Rio Grande, &c. By MRS. EGBERT L. VIELÉ. 12mo. Muslin, price $1 00.

ETHEL'S LOVE-LIFE.

By MRS. M. J. M. SWEAT. "Rarely has any recent work expressed the intenseness of a woman's love with such hearty *abandon*." 12mo. Muslin, price $1 00.

STORIES FOR CHILDHOOD.

By AUNT HATTY (Mrs. Coleman). Beautifully bound in cloth, gilt, and profusely illustrated. Put up in boxes containing 12 assorted volumes. Price per box, $4 00.

GOOD CHILDREN'S LIBRARY.

By UNCLE THOMAS. A dozen charming stories, beautifully illustrated; bound in cloth, gilt backs. Put up in boxes containing 12 assorted volumes. Price per box, $4 00.

SOUTHWOLD.

By MRS. LILLIE DEVEREUX UMSTED. "A spirited and well drawn Society novel—somewhat intensified but bold and clever." 12mo. Muslin, price $1 00.

DOESTICKS' LETTERS.

Being a compilation of the Original Letters of Q K. P. DOESTICKS, P. B. With many comic tinted illustrations by John McLenan. 12mo. Muslin, price $1 00.

PLU-RI-BUS-TAH.

A song that's by-no-author. *Not* a parody on "Hiawatha." By DOESTICKS. With 150 humorous illustrations by McLenan. 12mo. Muslin, price $1 00

THE ELEPHANT CLUB.

An irresistibly droll volume. By DOESTICKS, assisted by KNIGHT RUSS OCKSIDE, M.D. One of his best works. Profusely illustrated by McLenan. Muslin, price $1 00.

THE WITCHES OF NEW YORK.

A new humorous work by DOESTICKS; being minute, particular, and faithful Revelations of Black Art Mysteries in Gotham. 12mo. Muslin, price $1 00

TWO WAYS TO WEDLOCK.

A Novellette. Reprinted from the columns of Morris & Willis' *New York Home Journal.* 12mo. Handsomely bound in muslin. Price $1 00,

THE SPUYTENDEVIL CHRONICLE.

A sparkling Novel of young Fashionable Life in New York; a Saratoga Season; Flirtations, &c. A companion to the "Potiphar Papers." Muslin, price 75 cents.

ROMANCE OF A POOR YOUNG MAN.

From the French of OCTAVE FEUILLET. An admirable and striking work of fiction. Translated from the Seventh Paris edition. 12mo. Muslin, price $1 00.

THE CULPRIT FAY.

By Joseph Rodman Drake. A charming edition of this world-celebrated Faery Poem. Printed on colored plate paper. Muslin, 12mo. Frontispiece. Price, 50 cts.

THE NEW AND THE OLD;

Or, California and India in Romantic Aspects. By J. W. Palmer, M.D., author of "Up and Down the Irrawaddi." Abundantly illustrated. Muslin, 12mo. $1,25.

UP AND DOWN THE IRRAWADDI;

Or, the Golden Dagon. Being passages of adventure in the Burman Empire. By J. W. Palmer, M.D., author of "The New and the Old." Illustrated. Price, $1,00.

ERIC; OR, LITTLE BY LITTLE.

A Tale of Roslyn School. By F. W. Farrar (Fellow of Trinity College, Cambridge). An admirable picture of inner school life. Muslin, 12mo. Price, $1,00.

RECOLLECTIONS OF THE REVOLUTION.

A private manuscript journal of home events, kept during the American Revolution by the Daughter of a Clergyman. Printed in unique style. Muslin. Price, $1,00

HARTLEY NORMAN.

A New Novel. "Close and accurate observation, enables the author to present the scenes of everyday life with great spirit and originality." Muslin, 12mo. Price, $1,00.

BORDER WAR.

A Tale of Disunion. By J. B. Jones, author of "Wild Western Scenes." One of the most popular books ever published in America. Muslin. 12mo. Price, $1,25.

www.ingramcontent.com/pod-product-compliance
Lightning Source LLC
LaVergne TN
LVHW010248110826
845151LV00004B/1419
9781425522711